JAY NEWMAN is associate professor of philosophy at the University of Guelph.

Religious intolerance is very old and widespread – a phenomenon of a highly distinctive nature which defies reduction to a simpler kind of vice. Methods of achieving religious tolerance have long been in dispute because there is much confusion about its nature.

In this book, Professor Newman attempts to clarify the concept of religious tolerance in a way that other recent philosophical studies have clarified such concepts as justice, freedom, and equality. While there is a great deal of literature on theological, psychological, sociological, and political aspects of the problem, little has been said about the more fundamental ethical and epistemological issues that arise from philosophical reflection on religious competition and conflict.

Newman addresses such questions as: How does religious intolerance differ from religious prejudice? Does being tolerant require commitment to relativism, pluralism, secularism, or universalism? Can a State live up to its promise to allow its citizens freedom of religion? Is intolerance a vice or a deep-rooted psychosis? Is it an inevitable by-product of educational socialization?

In shedding light on these and related problems, offering tentative solutions, and drawing on the writings of such philosophers as Aristotle, Aquinas, Spinoza, and Hume and such modern thinkers as Gordon Allport, Ronald Knox, and Walter Lippmann, *Foundations of Religious Tolerance* will assist clergymen, scholars, and laymen in their attempts to promote social harmony and mutual understanding among people of different faiths.

This book will be especially useful in university courses and other programs in religious studies, philosophy, psychology, and sociology of religion, or that deal with prejudice and discrimination.

JAY NEWMAN

Foundations of
Religious Tolerance

UNIVERSITY OF TORONTO PRESS
Toronto Buffalo London

© University of Toronto Press 1982
Toronto Buffalo London
Printed in Canada

ISBN 0-8020-5591-5 (cloth)
ISBN 0-8020-6507-4 (paper)

Canadian Cataloguing in Publication Data

Newman, Jay, 1948–
  Foundations of religious tolerance
  Includes index.
  ISBN 0-8020-5591-5 (bound) ISBN 0-8020-6507-4 (pbk.)
  1. Religious tolerance. 2. Religious liberty.
  I. Title.
  BR1610.N48   261.7'2   C82-094051-8

This book has been published with the help of a grant from the Canadian
Federation for the Humanities, using funds provided by the Social Sciences
and Humanities Research Council of Canada, and a grant from the
Publications Fund of University of Toronto Press.

To my mother, Kate Newman

Acknowledgments

I am grateful to the publishers of the following books for permitting me to quote from copyrighted material: Gordon W. Allport, *The Nature of Prejudice* (Cambridge [and Reading], Mass: Addison-Wesley Publishing Company 1954 [© 1954, 1958, 1979]); Walter Lippmann, *A Preface to Morals* (New York: Macmillan 1929 [copyright renewed 1957]); R.A. Knox, *The Belief of Catholics* (London: Ernest Benn 1927). Earlier versions of some portions of this book have appeared in journal articles, and I am grateful to the editors and publishers of the periodicals in which they appeared for permitting me to make use of this material: 'Metaphysical Relativism,' *Southern Journal of Philosophy*, 12 (1974), 435–48; 'Popular Pragmatism and Religious Belief,' *International Journal for Philosophy of Religion*, 8 (1977), 96–110 (published by Martinus Nijhoff Publishers B. V.); 'Education as Civilization,' *Journal of Educational Thought*, 11 (1977), 203–12; 'Judaism as Racism: A Refutation of Berdyaev,' *Canadian Zionist*, 46, no. 2 (1977), 9–10, 14–15; 'Exclusive Salvation,' *Sophia*, 17, no. 3 (1978), 16–26; 'The Idea of Religious Tolerance,' *American Philosophical Quarterly*, 15 (1978), 187–95; 'Prejudice as Prejudgment,' *Ethics*, 90 (1979), 47–57 (published by the University of Chicago Press). Chapter 5 incorporates a revised version of part of my paper, 'The Ethics of Proselytizing,' in John King-Farlow ed., *The Challenge of Religion Today* (New York: Science History Publications 1976), one of the volumes in the Canadian Contemporary Philosophy Series. I am very grateful to John St James and R.M. Schoeffel of the University of Toronto Press for their generous attention to the manuscript and their kindness to the author.

Contents

FOUNDATIONS OF RELIGIOUS TOLERANCE

1

The concept of religious tolerance

Much has been said and written about love, comparatively little about hate. We generally prefer not to think about what is evil, ugly, or unpleasant. Those preoccupied with the negative things in life, the violence and injustice and inhumanity, become infected with a sickness of the soul, the sickness of cynicism and despair. But sometimes we have to think about hate; for how else can we forge the weapons with which to fight it?

Intolerance is the most persistent and the most insidious of all sources of hatred. It is perhaps foremost among the obstacles to civilization, the instruments of barbarism. And it has been able to do its damage largely because men have never understood it or made a strong enough effort to understand it. Thousands of years after the advent of Judaism and Christianity, Buddhism and classical philosophy, we look around the globe and see an unhealthy share of discrimination and prejudice, racism and bias, oppression and contempt. The hostility and persecution go on and on, uninterrupted, in Belfast and Cape Town, Odessa and Chicago, in the local university and that exclusive country club on the other side of town. And as intolerance carries on with unabated force, we go on with the business of living; we sit at our cocktail parties, discussing the latest film or fashion, our new domestic problem or neurosis. We have conquered morbidity by ignoring it. We have our own problems; how can we bother listening to the silence of Auschwitz?

But sometimes we have to think about intolerance, and in the pages that follow, that is what we are going to do. We shall be considering the most complex form of intolerance, religious intolerance, the kind that vitiates our highest spiritual ideals. But to lighten our burden, we shall approach the subject indirectly; we shall focus most of our attention on the other and positive side of the coin, religious tolerance.

4 Foundations of Religious Tolerance

TOLERANCE

We shall begin by considering what men mean when they talk about
'religious tolerance.' Eventually we are going to find that most men are
not very clear about the nature of religious tolerance, and that their
conceptual confusions are reflected in their everyday discourse. So we
are going to have to arrive at an idea of religious tolerance which is more
profound and more internally consistent than that of the man in the
street.

The word 'tolerence' is a noun that corresponds to the verb 'tolerate.'
Men can tolerate all sorts of things. My teachers often complained about
the widespread willingness to tolerate arrogance and bad manners.
They could not tolerate such things. My mother claims that she cannot
tolerate all of my father's eccentricities. My physician told me many
years ago that I did not have a tolerance for penicillin. I often hear
relatives say that a certain aunt is intolerant with regard to blacks and
certain immigrants. So there are many kinds of tolerance and intolerance which have nothing to do with religion or religious belief. When
people talk about tolerance in these different senses, they are always
speaking about a kind of acceptance or endurance. My mother cannot
accept or endure some of my father's eccentricities, and she invariably
reacts to them. People who cannot tolerate bad manners cannot accept
or endure them, cannot bear them, and they show us that they cannot
by reacting strongly to them. I cannot accept or endure penicillin in that
I react to it with a variety of unpleasant side-effects. So to tolerate
something is to accept or endure that thing without reacting strongly to
it. To tolerate it is to bear it, to put up with it. It is not to like or respect
the thing. My mother does not like *any* of my father's eccentricities or
respect him for them. But some of them she tolerates. I do not like bad
manners or respect people for them. But usually I tolerate bad manners.
Often we do not react strongly to things we do not like or respect people
for.

To say that tolerance is a kind of acceptance or endurance is to reveal
little, for in this context at least, 'acceptance' and 'endurance' are
themselves nebulous terms. One does not accept someone's eccentricities in precisely the same way as he accepts a gift, an invitation, a
challenge, or a belief. The kind of acceptance involved here must be
understood in terms of the criterion of reaction. Sometimes we speak of
people as tolerant or intolerant on the basis of whether their likes and
dislikes are reasonable or unreasonable. But for practical purposes, the

test and determinant of tolerance and intolerance is in action, specifically in the way a person reacts to whatever he is or is not tolerating. Moral evaluations are essentially evaluations of behaviour rather than opinion; opinions are only relevant to morality when they influence conduct. Few of us believe that a nasty thought is as bad as a nasty deed; and in any case, we do not possess the power to delve into the recesses of the minds of other men. So when my mother says that she cannot tolerate my father's snoring, she is not saying that she has an irrational dislike for it; rather, she is saying that she has come to the point where she must take action to prevent her being disturbed by it. By not having reacted to it up to this point she has accepted or endured it.

Another condition of tolerance is that it is half-hearted; it is the acceptance in one sense of something one does not accept in another sense. We do not *merely* tolerate those things we like, love, or approve of; tolerance involves acceptance or endurance of something that one has a negative attitude towards. Every act of tolerating involves an underlying wish that things were different. One cannot both like and tolerate the same thing. There are, of course, different degrees of disapproval. A child who tolerates sherbet when he really wants ice cream does not necessarily dislike sherbet in any absolute terms, but he would prefer ice cream to sherbet, and so he is merely tolerating the sherbet because he disapproves of it or dislikes it relatively to what he might have been given for dessert. We often tolerate things we do dislike in absolute terms; but often we tolerate things we dislike in a more limited sense, in that we recognize that they fall short of our grandest desires or expectations.

When we consider ordinary discourse, we are reminded that there are two different nouns corresponding to the verb 'tolerate' – 'tolerance' and 'toleration.' The latter seems to have a broader application; it refers to any instance of tolerating. But 'tolerance' is more closely related to the adjective 'tolerant.' Toleration is merely *instantiated* in each instance of toleration; the term is entirely behavioural. Tolerance is *expressed* as well as instantiated in tolerant actions. A person can be tolerant on one occasion and intolerant on another. But most of us believe that some men are generally tolerant while others are not. 'Tolerance,' then, unlike 'toleration,' is often seen as a character trait, a disposition, and usually as that kind of disposition that we call a 'virtue.' In this sense, tolerance is like courage or temperance, and we praise a man for being tolerant in the same spirit as we praise him for being courageous or temperate.

If we think of tolerance as a virtue, then the concept of tolerance has a normative aspect as well as a descriptive one. To say that a person is tolerant is often to make a value judgment about him in addition to describing him. The concept of tolerance, however, does not necessarily or always have a normative aspect. A person may criticize someone, even himself, for merely tolerating what he should strongly approve of or respect. And a person may also criticize himself or someone else for tolerating something that should not be tolerated (for instance, as when injustice or arrogance is tolerated). But when we think of tolerance as a virtue, as we often do, we are thinking of it strictly as tolerance of *what ought to be* tolerated.

We now have a sort of 'definition' of 'tolerance,' an analysis of the term based on a perception of how it is used in everyday discourse. 'Tolerance' is not a technical term in the way that, say, 'ontological' or 'ionization' is; it is a word used in restaurants and living rooms by businessmen and lawyers, carpenters and typists. We only have a working definition, and we shall have to take a closer look at the concept of tolerance. But we have found at least this much: tolerance involves tolerating, that is, accepting, enduring, bearing, putting up with; it involves acceptance in the sense of refraining from any strong reaction to the thing in question; it is half-hearted, an attitude towards something that is not liked, loved, respected, or approved of; and it is often, though not always, understood as a praiseworthy act or virtue.

TOLERANCE AND RELIGION

Having considered the concept of tolerance, we are now in a better position to understand the idea of *religious* tolerance and the fundamental confusions that have arisen with regard to it. But I do not think it prudent for us to attempt to analyse religion in the way that we have just analysed tolerance. 'Religion' is no more technical a term than 'tolerance'; it too has a place in everyday discourse. Yet it is obviously one of those strange terms that suggest very different things to different people. Religion clearly involves beliefs about the 'spiritual' – whatever that may be – and actions based on such beliefs. Most of us tend to associate religion with certain communities of believers (for instance, the Jewish, Roman Catholic, or Presbyterian), each of which is made up of individuals who share a commitment to certain metaphysical beliefs about the ultimate nature of reality and certain ethical principles concerning how to live. Some of us believe that belonging to a particular

community of believers is not an essential condition of religion; some
believe that a man can be described as 'religious' even if he does not
believe in the existence of a consciousness higher than that of human
beings. Some identify religion with a kind of symbolic thinking, while
others associate it with ritual or prayer. Some have even argued that
religion is indistinguishable from certain traditional forms of speculative philosophy. I shall resist the temptation to offer my own definition
of 'religion' so as not to alienate or offend any readers who profoundly
disagree with me in this matter. I am going to assume that our concepts
of religion have enough in common to render the rest of this discussion
intelligible. However, for reasons that will become apparent, I am going
to emphasize the metaphysical and ethical content of religion.

Religious tolerance is tolerance of one or more of the following:
religious (metaphysical, ethical) beliefs, religious actions (rituals or
any other actions based on religious beliefs), or religious people (people
who hold religious beliefs and engage in religious actions). Religious
tolerance may also be involved in those cases where religious men
tolerate non-religious things. And so religious tolerance may take
several forms. A non-religious person may tolerate some, most, or all
religious beliefs, actions, or people; a religious person may tolerate
some, most, or all non-religious beliefs, actions, or people; or – and here
is the case we usually think of – a religious person may tolerate some,
most, or all religious people who do not share *his particular* religious
beliefs or ways of acting, or he may tolerate some, most, or all of their
religious beliefs and actions.

Most of the confusion about the nature of religious tolerance has
stemmed from a misunderstanding of what is involved in tolerating a
religious *belief.* It is the element of belief that makes religious tolerance
more complex than racial tolerance or tolerance of bad manners. For it
is widely and mistakenly believed that tolerating a belief is primarily a
matter of making a judgment about the content of that belief. Some
people seem to think of tolerating as a propositional attitude. But
tolerating a belief is primarily a matter of making a judgment about
specific cases of *believing.*

Let me explain this obscure thesis by means of an illustration. Roman
Catholics believe that there is one God who exists in three eternal
persons (the Father, the Son, the Holy Spirit). This proposition – let us
call it p – is unquestionably one of the central propositions of the
Catholic's creed. But p is rejected not only by atheists but by Jews and
certain Christians (for instance, Unitarians). What is involved when an

atheist, Jew, or Unitarian tolerates the Catholic's belief in p, or when the Catholic tolerates someone's belief in not-p (that is, in p's falseness)? Clearly it is not proposition p that is being tolerated by the Unitarian or the Jew. For the Unitarian or the Jew, p is *false*, as false as the proposition that God has a body or the proposition that the moon is made of green cheese. From an ethical and an epistemological point of view, the Unitarian's 'attitude' towards p is wholly negative; he doubts p, and he believes that those who believe p are seriously mistaken. And the falsehood of p is something the Unitarian or Jew takes very, very seriously; he may well be prepared to burn at the stake or suffer other hardships rather than publicly affirm belief in p. So in tolerating the Catholic's belief in p, the Unitarian or Jew is not in any way mitigating his judgment about the *content* of p, his judgment that p is false. Nor is he implying that he considers p more reasonable than alternative propositions accepted by atheists, pantheists, or witch doctors. Nor is he even indicating that he is not bothered by the fact that Catholics and others believe p. He is not adopting a special attitude towards p; rather, he is adopting a certain attitude towards the Catholic's *believing* of p.

There is simply no way that a Unitarian or Jew or atheist can 'accept' or 'endure' p; he *rejects p*, and he believes that the Catholic ought to reject it too. Tolerating a religious belief, then, does not involve a half-hearted acceptance or endurance of the belief *in itself*, but rather it involves acceptance or endurance of *someone's holding* that belief, that is, of a certain case of believing. Now let me explain why I think this is so important. In recent years, philosophy and the social sciences have been infected by the pernicious doctrine of relativism, a doctrine we shall be considering over and over again in the course of our inquiry. From a relativistic standpoint, it can make sense to put up with beliefs one dislikes, but one of the results of the rise of relativism has been the increasing popularity of the view that tolerating someone's religious beliefs involves *respecting* his religious beliefs. In effect, to hold such a view of tolerance is to see tolerating as a kind of propositional attitude.

But how can the Unitarian or Jew or atheist respect a proposition like p when he considers p to be false and is even prepared to suffer great hardships rather than affirm belief in p? Many Jews and other 'disbelievers' have been prepared to accept and endure torture and extreme privation rather than accept belief in or public commitment to p. The plurality of religions is itself a testament to the seriousness with which Jews, Unitarians, and others look upon the difference between the content of p and the content of not-p. Nor is the 'disbeliever' likely to see p as a doctrine 'almost, but not quite as good' as not-p, in the way that

the young child tolerates sherbet because it is almost, but not quite a good as ice cream. Proposition *p* does not represent some middle ground between not-*p* and some other proposition. For the Jew, Unitarian, and atheist, *p* is false, and its falsity is not something to be taken lightly.

Consider this matter from another perspective. For those who have been bitten by the bug of relativism, the Catholic, Jew, and atheist can only be regarded as tolerant if they regard belief in *p* as not significantly better or significantly worse than belief in not-*p*. Such a view indirectly impugns all religious teachings and suggests that they are not nearly as important as has traditionally been thought. But this view not only conflicts with the actual nature of religious commitment but also conflicts with the true nature of tolerance. For think back to a point we considered earlier. Tolerance, by its very nature, is half-hearted, and it involves acceptance of something one has a negative attitude towards. Catholics believe that Jews ought to believe *p*; and Jews believe that Catholics should not believe *p*. For even if they profess to be uninterested in what other men believe, the Catholic has a negative attitude towards not-*p*, while the Jew has a negative attitude towards *p*; but the Catholic or Jew professes to *be* concerned with the interests of other men, and he must also believe that it is very much in his fellow ma interest to hold religious beliefs that are true. The Catholic has, then, at least in an abstract sense, a negative attitude towards the Jew's believing not-*p*, while the Jew has a negative attitude towards the Catholic's believing *p*. Now, we have just seen that it is one thing to accept someone's holding a certain belief and quite another thing to accept the belief per se; and to regard a belief as false or unreasonable is certainly to reject it in a fundamental sense of the word.

Here is a second point: if the Jew or Unitarian believes that *p* is no less (or more) true than not-*p*, and if he regards belief in *p* as neither significantly better nor significantly worse than belief in not-*p*, is he capable of merely *tolerating* someone's belief in *p*? Is he capable of being only half-hearted in his acceptance of the Catholic's believing in *p*? Can the Jew or Unitarian even remain a zealous, devout Jew or Unitarian if he believes that his most basic religious beliefs are no better, by any standard, than anyone else's? The fact is that most religious believers regard their religious beliefs as true; moreover, for a variety of reasons they believe that it is moral and prudent to hold the religious beliefs that they hold. And it is hard to disapprove of a belief, or of someone's holding a belief, when one feels that the belief is in no way inferior to one's own.

So it would seem that tolerating a religious belief is not primarily a

matter of making a judgment about the content of that belief. It is not acceptance of a belief per se or even acknowledgment of the relative reasonableness of the belief; rather, 'tolerating' is acceptance of someone's holding a belief that one considers to be significantly inferior to one's own alternative belief, if not by the standard of truth or falsity, then by some other standard. However, tolerating a religious belief is *secondarily* a matter of making a judgment about that belief's content. For one may be able to endure the company of a Jew or Catholic or Unitarian and yet be unable to endure the company of one who publicly affirms his belief in the main doctrines of, say, Satanism or atheistic communism. And the fact is that many people are not even capable of enduring the company of those who believe in Judaism or Catholicism or some non-materialistic form of atheism. Indeed, the question arises as to how one *can* tolerate someone's believing a proposition that he himself regards as both false and important. For even if tolerating someone's religious beliefs does not require our looking favourably upon the content of his beliefs, our accepting his right to believe whatever he wants to believe is not in itself an easy thing to do.

SOURCES OF RELIGIOUS INTOLERANCE

In considering the question of why men have so much trouble tolerating the religious 'believings' of other men, we must recognize that some of the sources of intolerance, such as superstition and ethnocentrism, are wholly irrational. The primary way to deal with irrationality is to discourage it by promoting rationality through education. One cannot argue intelligently with a man who has no respect for logic and dialogue, and often we have to use force to prevent bigoted fanatics from creating havoc; but the ultimate answer to superstition and irrationality must be education. There are, however, certain rational forms of intolerance, and these pose special problems.

Some cynics take solace in the fact that the propensity to intolerance is rooted in human nature. But so what? The propensity to most vices is rooted in human nature, yet most vices can be overcome. So it is worth our while to consider the different ways in which 'human nature' leads men to intolerance. The rational sources of religious intolerance are essentially of three kinds: philosophical, altruistic, and prudential. That is, men seek to change the religious beliefs of other men because they are concerned with either truth or their fellow man's welfare or their own welfare.

Consider the first kind. Many of us are willing to allow people to live by their illusions as long as these people do no harm. We accept certain illusions as innocent, innocuous; in fact, people who believe in elves and fairies can be rather charming, refreshingly different. There are some people, however, who believe that no illusions are innocuous. These are the people who believe that one ought to believe only what is *true*, no matter what the consequences. They are not concerned with utilitarian considerations, with the greatest happiness for the greatest number; they are interested in 'Truth for Truth's sake.' Those among them who also believe that their own religious beliefs are true are inevitably motivated to react strongly to what they consider to be religious illusions. They are relatively unimpressed by the fact that such 'illusions' may have pragmatic or psychotherapeutic value. For them, value is of secondary importance where truth is at stake.

Now, it is very hard for such people to be tolerant, especially if they believe that religious beliefs are more important than most beliefs. A few of them may be content with recognizing how vicious people are in taking truth so lightly, but most of them will react strongly to what they take to be religious illusions. And the latter will not regard themselves as intolerant, for they will be quick to point out that a truly tolerant man does not tolerate what ought not to be tolerated. How should we deal with such people? How can we make them act in the spirit of what *we* call 'tolerance'? For one thing, we might attack their basic principle that truth, in the last analysis, is all that matters. We might argue that love and goodwill and the general happiness are all as important as true belief. Or we might argue that truth will not change no matter what we fallible mortals happen to believe. But we are already treading on dangerous ground when we give this kind of argument; we are heading straight for relativism. We are beginning to suggest that religious 'truth' is not like scientific truth and is not as solid or as important as the latter. We must not take lightly the differences between any two religious faiths, for to do so would be to desecrate the memory of the millions of people who have been willing to suffer and die for their faith, and it would also be to underestimate the seriousness of their persecutors and of all religious men.

One invariably runs into trouble when one begins to take truth lightly. It is safer and wiser to challenge the self-professed 'defender' of truth than to challenge truth itself. It is one thing to love truth for its own sake and quite another thing to profess to love it for its own sake, and if one carefully examines the actions of most of these self-professed 'defenders' of truth, one notices that there are few modern Aristotles.

We can trust Aristotle when he tells us that he loves truth and wisdom and is prepared to devote his life to them. But what about these young Mormons and Jehovah's Witnesses who come proselytizing? How much have they studied? How many hours a day do they devote to reflection and contemplation? How is it that these missionaries who speak of truth can see themselves as wiser than learned doctors and professors, philosophers and theologians? We should be patient and rational in dealing with these defenders of truth, but we must demand that they be patient and rational too. If we can show a self-professed defender of truth-for-its-own-sake that what *he* regards as true is not *obviously* true, he will not react so strongly to the 'believings' of other men. That is, he will become more tolerant.

The altruistic bigots are the ones who want to save us. They cannot tolerate our doing ourselves harm. They are not necessarily worried about truth for its own sake. They are worried about *us*, our souls, our spiritual lives. Sometimes they will go to great extremes to save us; they will torture us, burn us at the stake, deny us freedom of choice. How can we get such men to tolerate what they perceive as our 'doing ourselves harm'? We can begin by suggesting to them that in harming our bodies or preventing us from accepting the dictates of our reason or our conscience, they are harming us more than we can ever harm ourselves. But we have to be careful here; we do not want to be put in the position of having to defend the thesis that physical, temporal things are more important than spiritual, eternal things. For even if one regards this thesis as true, and I myself do not, one must be mindful of the outlook of the persecuting altruist. So instead, we can point to the teaching and example of great religious leaders like Moses and Buddha and Jesus, who do not take physical, temporal violence and oppression lightly. One is not 'witnessing' very well if one has to resort to murder and torture and the suppression of rational thought. The greatest of religious leaders have been teachers, not bullies. Besides, in preventing a man from *choosing* the right course, on the basis of insight and understanding, one may be preventing him from being saved. If nothing else, one is preventing him from making full use of his human powers, and so is doing him spiritual as well as physical damage. The persecuting altruist must be taught that what he regards as true is not as obviously true as he has believed, or at least not as obviously true to those of different backgrounds and perspectives as it is to him. He must be made to see that there are methods of witnessing that do not require the use of force (for instance, appealing to reason and setting a good example). He must be encouraged to pay more attention to those religious teachings that relate to the immorality of force, violence, and oppression. That is, he must be made to see that according to most great religious teachers, being tolerant is an important part of being religious. For tolerating 'believings' is itself an important part of tolerating people. And no major religion sanctions our treating human beings as anything less than human beings.

And so we come to the intolerance of the prudent man. Many people regard the religious 'outsider' as a threat to the unity of their religious community. They do not so much object to the outsider's beliefs as to his actions, his behaviour. When children see how the outsider behaves, their respect for the religion of their parents often wanes. They begin to grasp the concept of alternatives, to ask questions, to challenge authority. If the outsider quietly held his personal beliefs but acted as everyone else does, he would not be a threat to the unity of the community. But religious belief usually gives rise to a special pattern of living; a major part of religious doctrine is ethical, normative, and prescribes how we ought to behave. Now, the best way to stop a man from acting strangely is to stop him from thinking strangely. In short, the prudent man is not so much worried about truth or the outsider's soul as he is about his own welfare and the welfare of his co-religionists; it is certain religious actions, certain religious behaviour, that he cannot tolerate, and if he tries to stop the outsider from believing what he believes, it is because he sees the outsider's 'subversive' actions as rooted in his beliefs.

The attitude of the prudent bigot clearly is not in the spirit of tolerance. We can try to persuade the prudent bigot that the use of force should be a last resort, that the truth of his beliefs is not all that obvious, and so on; but ultimately we must come face to face with the attitude itself. For to those who have such an attitude and fear the spread of apostasy, secularism, and materialism, force may well appear to be the only efficient resort left open. What one man sees as freedom, another may well see as licence, and if a member of the majority believes that the members of a small cult are, by their actions, setting a bad example for the young, disrupting established social institutions, and destroying the unity of the community, it is hard for him to accept or endure their religious actions without reacting strongly.

Any ideological pluralism, and especially a religious one, does take its toll on the laws of a society, which usually come to reflect that 'lowest common denominator' of ethical principles accepted by members of *all* the major groups making up the society. Most of us find the idea of a theocracy unattractive, and we know that theocracies are not governed by God but by dictators. We also know that living in a pluralistic society does not necessarily destroy one's religious faith or that of one's children. But consider the other side of the ledger. There can be no question that religious institutions have an importance in a theocracy (or even in most societies where there is an established state church) that they do not have in a society that is highly pluralistic and made up of several competing churches or communities of believers. There obviously can be no state church in a democratic society in which there is significant disagreement about what the state church should be. And when the church is separated from the state, people develop an allegiance to secular political symbols and institutions which to some extent supplants their prior allegiance to purely religious symbols and institutions. This kind of secularism does not necessarily give rise to materialism, but it often allows materialism to flourish in a way that theocracies do not. So we can see how we and our children and grandchildren do pay a price for today's tolerance; and we can see why people like the Amish are so concerned about keeping their children away from the corrupting influences of our 'liberal' society.

The kind of intolerance we have been considering is associated with 'conservatives.' But consider a related kind of intolerance stemming from prudence. Even in this relatively *liberal* society of ours, there are important limits to our tolerance, limits that are determined largely by prudence. Look at the case of the Jehovah's Witnesses. They have made many demands and often have been vindicated by the highest courts in the land. But even our most liberal leaders will only acquiesce to their requests *up to a point.*[1] If, however, there were fifty times as many Jehovah's Witnesses as there are now, our political leaders would have to lend them a more sympathetic ear. Indeed, many of our political leaders would be Jehovah's Witnesses themselves. Or look at the case of observant Jews, who try to live according to *halacha* or traditional rabbinic law. In our liberal society Jews can worship in their synagogues, celebrate their own holidays, send their children to Jewish schools, and so forth. But often they find that social institutions will not accommodate their special needs. For example, in small communities (and even large ones), they often have to work on their Sabbath; there is no attractive alternative. In any case, Jews and Jehovah's Witnesses, because of their numbers and influence, are a good deal better off than members of more exotic cults.

Now, the kind of prudence that I have just been talking about may seem very different from the first kind, the one related to fear. But in both cases members of religious minorities are being told, 'We will tolerate your religious actions and beliefs only as long as they do not come into conflict with any of our major institutions; when they do, it is you people who will have to do the accommodating.' The more liberal a society is, the fewer will be the institutions it regards as 'major' in this sense. But even in a liberal society, the member of a religious minority must know his place in order to survive, and he must be constantly mindful of the fact that his liberal neighbours will only tolerate so much and no more. In his defence, the liberal is apt to ask, 'How much, after all, can fairly be expected of us? We already allow members of minorities to do x, y and z.' It is not easy to answer such a question. At one time, members of religious minorities would have been happy if they were allowed to do just x; later they came to take their right to do x for granted, and petitioned for the right to do y; and so on. By some standards, a society is tolerant if it does not burn religious outsiders at the stake.

The religious intolerance that stems from prudential considerations is probably the most difficult kind with which to deal. The defensive liberal's question is a reasonable one: 'How much can fairly be expected of us?' How much should we expect a reasonable man to tolerate? Should he alter his entire life-style simply to accommodate the needs of Zoroastrians or moon-worshippers, or even Jews or Mormons or Presbyterians? Has he not the right to expect members of minorities to do the bulk of the compromising and accommodating? Equally serious questions are raised by the prudent conservative who fears that religious pluralism will eventually lead to social disunity and the breakdown of traditional ethical and religious values. Now, the conservative will only become more tolerant when he has been convinced that he should not perceive the existence of religious minorities as a serious threat to the fundamental policies and institutions of his society. So we have to get him to see that the principal threats to a religious way of life are internal weaknesses and the incompetence of its defenders. We also have to remind the conservative that it is dangerous to try to repress freedom of thought and freedom of choice, and that the price religious leaders pay for doing so is often a high one – that of alienating the more enlightened members of their flock. In other words, we have to show the conservative that prudence itself dictates that we be gentle and patient with outsiders and worry more about our own beliefs, actions, and institutions than about the threat posed by theirs. We cannot expect the conservative to regard the beliefs and actions of religious outsiders as healthy or positive; but we do have a right to expect him to react to their differences in a civilized, rational way. The prudent liberal's problem is harder to solve. He is pointing out to us that it is not clear where we should draw the line between what ought to be tolerated and what need not be tolerated.

INTOLERANCE AND UNWARRANTED FORCE

I have already noted that for practical purposes the test and determinant of tolerance and intolerance is in action; when we say that a man is 'intolerant,' we mean that he refuses to accept or put up with something he can and should accept. His refusal to accept that thing is *manifested* in his reaction to it. So we say that he is 'intolerant' when we see that he has 'reacted strongly' – too strongly – to the thing in question. To be intolerant is not simply to have an irrational dislike. A man who has an irrational dislike for chicken but is still willing to eat it when it is served to him at a dinner party tolerates chicken in a way that he does not tolerate, say, blue cheese, which he refuses to eat under any circumstances. So the concrete test and determinant of tolerance is in action or, more specifically, reaction. Besides, we cannot read other people's minds or even always take them at their word, and so if they do not react strongly to something, we have no good reason to believe that they are genuinely intolerant of it. In fact, people who profess to dislike, say, blacks but are outraged by the mistreatment of blacks are not as intolerant as they think they are.

'Reacting strongly' is a nebulous phrase; what one man regards as a strong reaction another may regard as a weak one. Most of us consider murder and torture to be very strong reactions. But in the last few centuries, religious intolerance has only rarely manifested itself in acts of murder and torture. (I wish I could say never, but I cannot.) It is still quite common for members of religious minorities to find themselves excluded from executive positions, professional schools, and private clubs. They find their children being ridiculed by playmates. They find their houses of worship defaced. They find local governments refusing to give their religious schools financial aid comparable to that received by the religious majority's schools. They find themselves helplessly bombarded with offensive religious propaganda. And they find themselves being ignored or avoided in certain social circles. How much of this reaction is strong enough to qualify as a manifestation of intolerance?

One way in which this question might be answered is by applying a utilitarian standard. According to utilitarianism, the reaction is too strong (and hence wrong or bad) when it tends to increase the total general unhappiness. The right action or reaction is the one that is conducive to the greatest happiness for the greatest number of people. But utilitarianism has its weaknesses. Say, for example, that in having prevented a Roman Catholic from getting a job with their firm, fifty Protestant business executives have made themselves so happy that their total happiness outweighs the unhappiness of the Catholic, who can get a fairly good job with another firm. Even if the Catholic is not very unhappy, and even if the Protestant executives knew that the Catholic could get a good job with another firm, the executives reacted strongly enough to the Catholic's religion to qualify as intolerant men. Even if they thought that he would be happier in another job, they are still intolerant. So consider this second criterion: the reaction is too strong (and hence wrong) when it is based on seeing a man's religion as relevant to something to which it is not really relevant. Being a Catholic does not prevent a man from being a successful business executive. Still, 'relevance' is a vague term too. A genuinely religious person sees his religious beliefs as relevant to all aspects of his life. He does not stop being religious when he goes to work. The only people who talk about religion as being relevant in only certain contexts are those who do not take religion very seriously. So while it is obvious that a Catholic can be a good business executive, we should not draw the empty inference that being tolerant is a matter of recognizing when religion is 'relevant.' We need a more specific and more profound criterion.

In some of my earlier comments, I associated 'strong reaction' with the use of force. To force someone to do something is to make him do that thing *against his will*. (To prevent him from doing what he wants to do is also to use force against him; it is to force him, against his will, not to do something.) There are degrees of force: one can physically control a man's arms and legs in such a way that he cannot do anything but what the controller wants; or one can give the man a queer sort of 'choice' – 'Do such-and-such or we will torture your wife and children (or take away your job, exclude you from the club, harass you, and so on).' To force someone to do something is to deprive him of a certain degree of *freedom*, which, understood in a broad sense, is nothing more than *the ability to do what one wants*. (People can be conditioned to want very little, and these people will consider themselves very free because their wants are easily satisfied. Other men will recognize, however, that such people have had their options severely restricted.) Freedom is a trans-cultural, universal ideal. In a society that is reasonably advanced on the scale of civilization, people are not allowed to do whatever they want. They cannot murder, steal, or rape without incurring the wrath of their fellow citizens. Freedoms conflict; if a man were free to kill anyone that he wanted to kill, he would be, in effect, free to rob other human beings of *their* basic freedoms. The maximum amount of freedom in a society is brought about only when *certain* freedoms are curtailed. So while force as a general rule deprives men of a certain degree of freedom, some force is warranted and, in the long run, actually promotes freedom.

Consider the difference between two members of a religious group who have very different methods of getting someone to adopt their religious way of life: the first uses force, while the second believes only in rational persuasion. The second man is not necessarily intolerant. He goes to the potential proselyte, treats him as an intelligent and rational human being, and tries to show him, by reasoning with him, that he should adopt a new way of life. He does not approve of the potential proselyte's present way of life; but he is prepared to accept or put up with it until he can rationally persuade the man to convert by an act of free will. He is reacting to something he dislikes and disapproves of; he is attempting to change the potential proselyte's way of life. But he is patient enough to accept the man's present way of life until that man chooses another of his own free will. The first man, however, does not take freedom as seriously. He reacts with force: violence, threats, deception. That he has turned to force is evidence that he is not patient enough to accept the potential proselyte's present way of life. His intolerance has manifested itself in his use of force. Notice that the difference between the two men has nothing to do with happiness or 'relevance,' except perhaps indirectly. It has to do with the nature rather than the circumstances of the reaction.

It is, of course, not easy to determine when the use of force is warranted and when it is not. If the only way we can prevent ritual human sacrifice is by using force, then we must use force. Still, those who would be tolerant should above all be concerned with freedoms that are (or should be) *rights*. When we exclude a man from a job or school, we are interfering with his freedom or right to work or learn. We are not interfering with his more basic right to live, and so we are not being as intolerant as a Torquemada. But we are being more intolerant than those who interfere only with his freedom to enjoy their company (assuming, of course, that he wants to enjoy their company). His freedom to enjoy their company has to be weighed against their freedom to associate only with those with whom they wish to associate; he may not have a 'right' to enjoy their company. But what freedom is the bigoted employer invoking? Or a Torquemada? Is the scale of freedoms anywhere near being balanced here?

We have gradually been building up an explanatory model, a theory of tolerance; let us look again at the new piece of our model. To tolerate something is to accept it, and the test or determinant of whether we accept it or not is in our reaction to it. A man can react to something that he does not like or approve of and yet still be prepared to accept it. He can try to change another man's religious opinions and yet refuse to use force. So not tolerating something involves only some reactions, 'strong' ones. In the case of religious tolerance, reactions are considered strong enough to be wrong when they involve unwarranted use of force. When we think of force, we think of violence, threats, and deception. But essentially, force is the restriction or denial of freedom, or of specific freedoms or rights. When we force someone to do something, we are making him do that thing against his will, and we are showing that in some sense we cannot tolerate or accept his not doing it; and when we force someone to refrain from doing something, we are showing that we cannot tolerate or accept his doing it. But when we describe a man as 'tolerant,' we usually mean that he tolerates all and only those things that ought to be tolerated. We do not regard a man as virtuous if he tolerates anything and everything. Some things should be tolerated and other should not be; sometimes the use of force is not only morally acceptable but morally advisable. Freedoms often conflict, and one freedom must be weighed against others. Also, freedom is just one of several fundamental trans-cultural, universal ethical ideals; others are love, justice, wisdom, peace, self-realization, prosperity, and so forth. Force is often warranted because freedom itself must be weighed against other ideals. Now, there is no simple formula that enables us to do all this weighing of freedoms against freedoms and ideals against ideals. The defensive liberal's problem still stands. But judgments about what ought to be tolerated are not made in a vacuum; they are made against the background of a broad, synoptic ethical code. Those who see judgments about what we should tolerate as wholly 'relative' or arbitrary are almost certainly committed to an extremely radical form of ethical relativism.

TOLERANCE AS A VIRTUE

When I say, 'My dentist is tolerant' or 'My dentist is a tolerant man,' I am praising him in roughly the same spirit as I praise him when I say that he is temperate or courageous. I am not only describing one of his characteristics; I am praising him, saying that he has a certain virtue. People have had all sorts of ideas about the nature of virtue, but none are more insightful than those of the ancient Greek philosophers, for whom a virtue was a disposition which helps or enables a man to achieve self-realization or self-fulfilment. Against hedonists and relativists, the most important philosophers of ancient Greece maintained that a human being has a 'function,' a destiny, and that a virtue helps him to realize it while a vice hinders him in his attempts to realize it. In his *Nicomachean Ethics*, Aristotle also argues that a virtue is a mean between two vices, the extreme of excess and the extreme of deficiency. And we can analyse the virtue of tolerance along these lines. For when we say that a man is tolerant, we are indicating that we believe that he has found the mean between too much tolerating and not enough tolerating. Remember that the word 'tolerance' is closely related to the word 'tolerant'; tolerance involves *being tolerant*. And while a man may be tolerant only on this or that particular occasion, some men seem to be disposed to be tolerant on all occasions. (One does not have to be born with such a disposition; a disposition can be cultivated.) But then, we do not call a man 'tolerant' if he accepts or endures everything. As Aristotle points out at the beginning of the third book of the *Nicomachean Ethics*, 'To endure the greatest indignities for no noble end or for a trifling end is the mark of an inferior person.'² So being tolerant does not involve tolerating everything; it is a matter of tolerating all things and only those things that ought to be tolerated, and, by implication, using force whenever it is warranted.

There are, however, some people who do not even tolerate those things that *should* be tolerated. If the man who tolerates too much represents the 'extreme of excess,' the man who does not tolerate enough represents the extreme of deficiency. Both men are vicious rather than virtuous. When we think of the 'intolerant' man, however, we only think of the man who represents the extreme of deficiency.

Here, then, is a problem in our everyday language that is the source of much of our confusion about the nature of tolerance. We think and speak of tolerance as a virtue, a mean between two extremes; but we think and speak of intolerance only as a vice of deficiency. What about the man who tolerates too much? If tolerance is a virtue, this man cannot be considered tolerant. We do not, however, ordinarily say that he is intolerant. And it even seems unfair to call such a man 'non-tolerant' when he tolerates even more than the tolerant man does. So let us call this man 'indiscriminately tolerant' or 'tolerant through weakness,' for we have to have some way of describing him, and he is clearly weak in the sense of putting up with too much, with things he should not accept. Being indiscriminately tolerant is one way of being 'morally weak.' The virtue of 'tolerance,' then, is a mean between 'intolerance,' the extreme of deficiency, and 'indiscriminate tolerance,' the extreme of excess, on a scale that depicts degrees of tolerating. Here we understand, of course, that the tolerant man tolerates those specific things that ought to be tolerated, not just a moderate number of things.

Few men are wholly virtuous or vicious, even with regard to a particular set of related dispositions. For example, a miser occasionally spends too much money on certain things, and often he spends just the right amount of money. When Aristotle introduced his model of the virtue as a mean, his main aim was to clarify the concept of a virtue. I have borrowed his model in order to clarify the concept of tolerance and show that tolerance can be analysed in roughly the same way as other virtues can.

TOLERANCE VS RELATIVISM: A PRELIMINARY NOTE

We shall be taking a very close look at 'relativism' later on. But even at this early stage of our inquiry, where we are simply considering the boundaries of the concept of tolerance, I cannot resist giving an early warning of the importance of distinguishing the tolerant person from the relativist.

A relativist is a person who believes that something important that is generally regarded as absolute or objective (for instance, an ethical value or a religious belief) is actually dependent on the background, character, or attitudes of particular individuals or societies. For the ethical relativist, for example, actions are not good or right *in themselves* but are good-for-so-and-so or right-as-perceived-by-so-and-so. There are even some thinkers who believe that there is no such thing as absolute or objective truth, that a proposition is never true *in itself* but is always true-for-so-and-so or true-as-perceived-by-so-and-so. One of the most important facts of recent intellectual history is that relativism has been becoming an increasingly popular theory.

Relativists often claim to be concerned with tolerance, and many of them defend relativism by arguing that it is the only epistemological theory that provides an adequate theoretical foundation for tolerance. When they talk about religion, many relativists argue along the following lines: religious beliefs are not really true or false in any absolute or objective sense; they are either speculations, hypotheses, presuppositions, or personal perspectives; and while some are incentives to morality and peace of mind in a way that others are not, all of the major beliefs of the major religions of the world have roughly the same moral, spiritual, and psychotherapeutic value; therefore, for the most part it is foolish to be intolerant or to use force in trying to prevent people from holding on to the religious beliefs they presently hold.

If we read between the lines, we see that a certain kind of relativist is actually a *critic* of the spirit of tolerance, not a defender. For if we take his epistemological position seriously, we have no reason or right to be half-hearted in our acceptance of the 'believings' of other men. We should not merely tolerate their beliefs but should look favourably on them, for they are as sound, by the significant moral and spiritual and psychotherapeutic standards, as our own. Such a relativist must view religious tolerance as a vestige of an absolutistic conception of religion. He usually considers mere tolerance unreliable and feels that there will only be peace among men of different faiths when these men come to look favourably on each other's religious beliefs. And why, he argues, shouldn't they look favourably on each other's religious beliefs when no major religious belief is substantially truer or better than any other?

The *pure* relativist is simply masquerading as the apostle of religious tolerance. He is not a tolerant man at all; he is an 'indiscriminately tolerant' man. He is willing to tolerate any kind of religious opinion or action, provided that it does not threaten *him*. For the *pure* relativist, the metaphysics of the tribal barbarians who practise voodooism is not substantially inferior to the metaphysics that underlies the religion of a civilized people. Most proponents of a relativistic approach to religion, however, are not pure relativists. They are seriously prepared to admit that some religions are superior to others. According to them, there are 'great' religions and not-so-great religions; the latter are significantly inferior to the former, but all of the former are equally acceptable. This modified relativism is an attractive doctrine. Its proponents are not nearly as morally weak as the pure relativists. But where are we to draw the mysterious line between 'great' religions and not-so-great ones? At what point does a religion suddenly become 'great' and as acceptable as other 'great' religions? Is it not possible that Lutheranism or Islam is just *slightly* superior to or inferior to Roman Catholicism or Anglicanism or Judaism? Certainly there is a common ethical code underlying the oldest and most famous ecclesiastical religions. But are there not significant distinctions between the ethical codes of the Lutheran, Catholic, and Jew? Is it not dangerous and inaccurate to suggest that the only important part of a religion is that which it has in common with all other established religions? And finally, are we to dismiss as misled all those martyrs who chose to suffer and die rather than embrace what they perceived as an idolatrous way of life?

If what I have said about the *concept* of religious tolerance is reasonably accurate, then we may infer that being tolerant does not require one to be a relativist. But relativism deserves more attention than we have just given it, as does the concept of religious tolerance, for the 'definition' of 'religious tolerance' that we have arrived at is far too abstract to be of any practical value.

2

The concept of religious prejudice

Most languages are rich in terminology for describing the various forms of human stupidity, and our own language is especially rich in terminology for describing unwarranted attitudes and behaviour towards one's fellow human beings. For in addition to speaking of intolerance, we speak of bigotry, discrimination, ethnocentrism, bias, racism, and prejudice. In everyday language we tend to blur the distinctions between one such attitude and another; most men of goodwill profess to be uniformly opposed to all of these attitudes and actions and see little point in dwelling on the nuances. It would be foolish and pretentious to offer precise definitions of terms that are essentially non-technical and abstract. Everyday language is not nearly as clear and precise as some academic pedants would have us believe. But some nuances are more important than we customarily allow. It is, after all, no coincidence that we use so many terms (with remarkably different etymologies) to refer to the attitudes and actions under consideration; and though it is wrong to identify a word's meaning with its etymology, it is also wrong to sit by passively as our language is gradually deprived of the little descriptive precision it has.

We customarily associate prejudice with intolerance, and with good reason. But there is an important difference between the concept of intolerance and the concept of prejudice: while both concepts tend to have normative or ethical significance, the former is primarily psychological and the latter is primarily epistemological. The intolerant person does not accept something; the prejudiced person pre-judges. Religious intolerance and religious prejudice belong to the same family of concepts, but each concept corresponds to a different aspect of religious hatred.

PREJUDICE AS PRE-JUDGMENT

In his famous study of prejudice, Gordon Allport, though a psychologist
by trade, devotes several passages to conceptual analysis, some of which
I shall now quote:

The word *prejudice*, derived from the Latin noun *praejudicium*, has, like most
words, undergone a change of meaning since classical times. There are three
stages in the transformation. 1 / To the ancients, *praejudicium* meant a
precedent – a judgment based on previous decisions and experiences. 2 / Later,
the term, in English, acquired the meaning of a judgment formed before due
examination and consideration of the facts – a premature or hasty judgment. 3 /
Finally the term acquired also its present emotional flavor of favorableness or
unfavorableness that accompanies such a prior and unsupported judgment.

Perhaps the briefest of all definitions of prejudice is: *thinking ill of others
without sufficient warrant*. This crisp phrasing contains the two essential
ingredients of all definitions – reference to unfounded judgment and to a
feeling-tone. It is, however, too brief for complete clarity.

In the first place, it refers only to *negative* prejudice. People may be
prejudiced in favor of others; they may think *well* of them without sufficient
warrant. The wording offered by the New English Dictionary recognizes positive
as well as negative prejudice: *A feeling, favorable or unfavorable, toward a
person or thing, prior to, or not based on, actual experience*. While it is
important to bear in mind that biases may be *pro* as well as *con*, it is none the less
true that *ethnic* prejudice is mostly negative ...

The phrase 'thinking ill of others' is obviously an elliptical expression that
must be understood to include feelings of scorn or dislike, of fear and aversion, as
well as various forms of antipathetic conduct: such as talking against people,
discriminating against them, or attacking them with violence.

Similarly, we need to expand the phrase 'without sufficient warrant.' A
judgment is unwarranted whenever it lacks basis in fact. A wit defined prejudice
as 'being down on something you're not up on.'[1]

Allport has described to us here how an ancient term has gradually
evolved to the point where it is now one of a constellation of terms for
describing unwarranted attitudes towards others. Consider these additional aspects of the definition of 'prejudice': 1 / There are special uses of
the term 'prejudice' in science and law (for instance, 'prejudice' as
damage), but they are not directly relevant to an understanding of
'prejudice' in the ordinary sense, in which it refers to an attitude (which

'includes' feelings and forms of conduct). 2/We generally think of prejudice as involving pre-judgments about *people*. We would understand what a man meant if he told us that he had a prejudice against wolves or even a prejudice against prunes; but such uses of 'prejudice' have come to seem metaphorical. We sometimes hear 'prejudice' used in this context: 'I only trust scientific method, but I am a scientist, so I suppose that I am a bit prejudiced.' The speaker here has not just pre-judged certain methods but has pre-judged people who use those methods (for instance, philosophers, astrologers). 3/Allport sees 'ethnic' prejudice as the most basic and most important kind of prejudice. But other forms of prejudice are equally important. Allport does not mean to play down the importance of religious prejudice; but he believes that most religious prejudice is actually nothing more than ethnic prejudice. Now, we have to remember that not all prejudice involves viewing individuals as members of groups. We tend to pre-judge people who are different from us in some obvious way, even when they do not 'represent' a group or class. If there were only one black or one Jew or one mentally retarded person in the world, he might still be the victim of prejudice, simply because he was so different from everyone else. But there is another reason why we should be careful not to overemphasize the importance of the ethnic form of prejudice. There is something distinctive about, say, religion, which suggests that it is unwise to compare attitudes about it to attitudes about race, language, national origin, and so forth. There is something profoundly wrong with Allport's thesis that religious prejudice is essentially no different than other forms of prejudice. But this is a point that we can return to later in the chapter. 4/Prejudice against a person is based on a negative attitude towards certain real or imagined *characteristics* of that person. Any characteristic can be frowned upon: belief, age, colour (of skin, hair, eyes), style of dress, ignorance of local custom, mannerism, vocation, and so forth.

Though prejudice is a certain kind of pre-judgment, we no longer use the term 'prejudice' to refer to any premature or hasty judgment. We make many unwarranted judgments that do not qualify as prejudices. When a petrologist or meteorologist comes to a false conclusion about rocks or weather because his evidence or data is inadequate, we do not see him as prejudiced. Nor do we see a man as prejudiced if he dislikes strawberry ice cream but can give no good reason for disliking it. Nor are we likely to regard a man as prejudiced if he decides, on the basis of flimsy evidence, that his aunt will adore the book that he bought her for her birthday. When we say that a person is prejudiced, we are saying that he has made a judgment on the basis of inadequate (or no) evidence; but we are also saying more. We are saying that he has an unwarranted attitude towards some person, an attitude that is itself based on an attitude towards certain characteristics of that person.

Since, in all cases of prejudice, a person, x, has a certain attitude towards (or feeling about) another person, y, an attitude based on x's attitude towards certain real or imagined characteristics of y, x is making more than one judgment. He is making a judgment about y; but he is also making one or more judgments about the real or imagined characteristics of y. Since x has pre-judged, at least one of his judgments has been made on the basis of inadequate (or no) evidence. But where does the pre-judgment come in? x may have wrongly perceived y as having characteristic k. But x may also have rightly perceived y as having characteristic k and wrongly perceived k as making y a bad person. x may dislike Jews because he wrongly perceives them as being communists. But he may also believe that Jews are evil simply because they do not accept the Christian faith. In either case, when we say that x is *intolerant*, we are saying that he ought to accept something he does not accept; we are making a value-judgment. But when we say that x is *prejudiced*, we are saying that he has made an empirical or logical error, that he does not have sufficient grounds for believing something that he believes. In other words, we are saying that in addition to being callous, mean, and inflexible, x is *ignorant*. Consider now the various circumstances under which he can be regarded as ignorant.

The simplest case is that in which x holds a false belief about y's characteristics. Anyone who has even dabbled in analytical epistemology knows that we must approach the concept of *adequate evidence* with fear and trembling; but all epistemologists agree that if someone believes something that is false, then no matter how good his evidence is, in an important sense that evidence is not adequate. So if x believes that since y is an Irish Catholic, y must be an alcoholic, x has clearly pre-judged. We can present x with evidence that not all Irish Catholics are alcoholics. We can show him that he has prematurely and hastily ascribed characteristic k to y, and that he has no right (at this point, at least) to dislike or look down on y on the *grounds* that y has characteristic k. If x refuses to take our evidence seriously, he is irrational; but whether or not he admits it, we can see that he has pre-judged, that his judgment about y was rooted at least partly in ignorance. When we think about prejudice, we ordinarily think of cases of this kind. The man who hates blacks 'because they are lazy' and hates Jews 'because they are dishonest in their business dealings' has pre-judged blacks and Jews on the basis of some flimsy evidence that they have characteristic k. Unfortunately, prejudice is not always so simple.

There are situations in which men do not have good reasons for holding the true beliefs they hold. One can have a true belief without having knowledge. Consider these two cases, First, a man grows up in a society where there are no Jews. All he knows about the Jews is what he has been told by others. The local missionary, the visiting merchant, and his grandfather have all told him that Jews are wicked, dangerous people. The books he has read have all put Jews in an unfavourable light. He has never met any Jews, although he has heard a rumour to the effect that the most despised man in his village, a deceitful peddler, has some 'Jewish blood.' Yet, though he cannot explain why, he has a 'feeling' that Jews are not nearly as wicked as they have been made out to be. Indeed, Jews are not as wicked as he has been taught to believe. But what evidence does he have to justify his rejection of the claims of respected community leaders like his grandfather and the local missionary? How can he be so arrogant as to dismiss as inaccurate everything that he has read about Jews in books? We can see that the judgment of the missionary and the merchant is unwarranted; but it is certainly not clear that our hero's favourable attitude is any more justified, even though it is true. It could be argued that he is not *prejudiced in favour* of the Jews because all men have a prima facie obligation to think favourably about those men whom they have not known personally. But does our hero have a prima facie obligation to think favourably of Huns and inquisitors, of Heliogabulus and his armies, of Mongol hordes? Does he even have a prima facie obligation not to think unfavourably of them?

Now consider a case involving a negative attitude. A young man who has grown up in Alabama has observed the racist Ku Klux Klan from a distance. He does not know much about the Klan; he is not familiar with their activities. He has heard members of the Klan make racist remarks, but he has also heard his own mother make such remarks. Yet, though he does not understand the symbolism of the white hoods and the burning crosses, he is antipathetic towards the Klansmen. They 'seem' sinister to him. He regards their rituals as 'ugly' and 'primitive.' This young man is right in believing that the Klansmen are evil people. But since he knows virtually nothing about the Klan's activities, his negative attitude is unwarranted. For all he *knows*, they might simply be members of some quaint religious cult. And so in a sense he has no more right to regard Klansmen as evil than he does to regard Yankees or Russians as evil.

In the two cases that we have just considered, there is pre-judgment with regard to people and their real or imagined characteristics. Many would argue that our two heroes are, in spite of their healthy intuitions, prejudiced. Yet, some would argue that they are not prejudiced. For when some people talk about prejudice, they have these additional conditions in mind: 1 / *false judgment*: a man can only be regarded as prejudiced if his belief is false, regardless of how much or how little evidence he possesses; 2 / *maleficence*: a man can only be regarded as prejudiced if his belief, when widely held, would be productive of bad or harmful consequences. We find ourselves confronted here with some of the blurry edges of the concept of prejudice. Some will argue that prejudice is judgment that falls short of knowledge; others will argue that prejudice is judgment that falls short of truth. Ignorance can be a matter of not knowing, but perhaps it can also be a matter of not being aware of the truth. The second additional condition is a utilitarian one. (We must not confuse maleficence with malevolence; it is not motives that we are concerned with here, but consequences.) Pro-prejudice can lead to unhealthy consequences; if a man is too philo-Semitic, he may end up being guilty of reverse discrimination against his fellow gentiles. But a man who believes, on the basis of flimsy evidence, that Jews are not necessarily bad people, or that Klansmen are evil and dangerous, is not holding a belief that, when held by many people, would be conducive to evil consequences.

Some want to emphasize the value of 'prejudice' as a purely descriptive term. Others, seeing that the term has come to have pejorative force, are inclined to take the utilitarian condition seriously and ask, 'What *practical value* is there in regarding a man as prejudiced when the opinions he holds are not only true but healthy and decent?' We can see that there are different ways in which prejudice can be 'unwarranted' or 'unjustified.' According to Allport, 'A judgment is unwarranted whenever it lacks basis in fact.' But it is not clear how we should evaluate evidence in relation to fact. Our two heroes did not have good grounds for holding the true beliefs they held; but though their evidence was limited, their opinions certainly did not lack 'basis in fact.' Was their ignorance the ignorance of prejudice? And if their opinions were healthy and decent, were those opinions not *ethically* warranted? A utilitarian can argue plausibly that in one sense a judgment is unwarranted when it lacks basis in *value*; and a pragmatist can argue with at least some plausibility that when one talks about whether a judgment is warranted, one should not erect a wall between fact-considerations and value-considerations.

We now come to the third kind of situation, that in which x rightly believes that y has characteristic k (or characteristics k_1, k_2, k_3, etc.) and makes a value-judgment about y on the basis of an inference, a value-judgment that liberal, broad-minded people find unacceptable. This kind of situation is very common, perhaps as common as that in which x makes a mistake about y's characteristics. Here are some examples. A certain Catholic knows that Jews do not accept Christ as their saviour (k_1), do not accept Catholic teaching on such moral issues as abortion and divorce (k_2), and are generally opposed to public aid to parochial schools (k_3). Notice that this Catholic has not made a mistake in ascribing k_1, k_2, and k_3 to Jews. He does not see Jews as communists, money-worshippers, or people who engage in ritual slaughter of young gentile children. He has his facts straight, at least in so far as the judgments that he has made about the *characteristics* of Jews are reasonable. But look at what he has chosen to infer from his facts: 'Since Jews do not accept Catholic teaching on moral issues, they are evil, dangerous people.' 'Since Jews do not accept Christ as their saviour, they should not be allowed to teach in schools with a predominantly Christian student body.' 'Since Jews are opposed to public aid to parochial schools, we should not accept them as immigrants to our country.'

If we regard this man as prejudiced, it is because we believe that his conclusions, his value-judgments, are pre-judgments. It is because we regard him as ignorant in believing that his facts *support* his value-judgments, and because we see him as having made an error in inference. It is interesting to consider the arguments that bigots give to justify their contention that, say, blacks or Puerto Ricans are 'generally' bad people. Sometimes they simply ascribe characteristics to blacks and Puerto Ricans that in reality do not characterize these people at all. But sometimes the premises of their inferences are true: 'There is a great deal of crime in black neighbourhoods.' 'The percentage of Puerto Ricans in prison is high, while the percentage of Puerto Ricans in university is low.' 'Many blacks are on public welfare.' The bigot has his facts straight here. If he infers that blacks are *lazy* or that Puerto Ricans have *inherent criminal tendencies*, then our disagreement with him is empirical, and we must try to show him that he has made at least one mistake in ascribing characteristics to these people. But if he infers that blacks are *bad* or that we *ought* to avoid contact with Puerto Ricans, then his conclusion is normative.

This kind of pre-judgment is more problematic than the others we have considered, and for a simple reason: moral knowledge is more mysterious than ordinary empirical knowledge. Epistemologists can say all sorts of reasonable things about empirical judgments, empirical evidence, deductive and inductive inferences. But as any student of moral philosophy knows, it is not completely clear how we go about inferring an 'ought' from an 'is,' a value-judgment from an empirical judgment. Philosophers still disagree bitterly about what ought to count as 'moral evidence.' How, then, can we go about convincing a bigot that his value-judgment is a pre-judgment? Look again at the kind of inference that we are confronted with. Our fanatic Catholic is convinced that Jews are bad people because they do not accept Christ as their saviour. If he is prejudiced, he must be pre-judging the Jews; he must be hastily or prematurely inferring that they are bad people. But *where* is he pre-judging? Remember that some of the most intelligent Christian thinkers have considered this inference plausible and valid. And why not? Who is to say that the proper criterion of 'bad' (or 'ought,' 'right,' 'should,' 'good,' 'wrong') is that of the 'liberal Establishment'? Of course, we can say *something* to the bigot; we can try to appeal to his sensitivity to, say, utilitarian or deontological considerations. We can argue that the Jews cannot be 'bad' when, for example, they give so much support to Christian charities. We can explain that if Catholics have no contact with Jews, they will miss out on all sorts of learning opportunities, and so on. The bigot may be impressed. But what if he is not a utilitarian? (If he is not, he is in good company; some of the most perceptive moral philosophers of our time have repudiated utilitarianism.)

So our third kind of pre-judgment is more troublesome than the others. We started out by considering pre-judgments that are false empirical judgments (for instance, 'All Irish Catholics are alcoholics,' 'If he is a Jew, he must be obsessed with money,' 'Blacks tend to be lazy'). We then considered pre-judgments that, thought not really evident to the particular judge, appear to be true and morally proper to the rest of us ('Jews are not necessarily bad people,' 'Klansmen are evil people'). Such pre-judgments are often normative judgments, but we did not worry about this fact, for we saw that they are neither false nor maleficent. But now we have something to worry about, for we find ourselves confronted with judgments that are both normative and objectionable.

NORMATIVE PREJUDICE

Those who simply dismiss prejudice as 'ignorance,' and do not consider how and why particular kinds of pre-judgment are rooted in ignorance, have trouble explaining some simple facts. One is that bigots are often highly intelligent men – scientists, poets, philosophers, theologians. Another is that those who are prejudiced often have had more personal experience with, say, blacks or Jews than unprejudiced men have had. We often hear the bigot remark, 'You don't know these people as well as I do; I have had to live with them.' Yet, in spite of their intelligence and experience, such bigots still seem to us to be 'ignorant,' no matter how much evidence they point to.

When someone argues that 'Catholics are bad people' or 'an Indian cannot be a good person,' the rest of us take some solace in reflecting on old maxims: 'No man is wholly good or evil,' 'One cannot generalize about human beings,' and so forth. But the bigot's normative pre-judgments can be specific and prescriptive. The 'intelligent' bigot argues along the following lines: 'I have known many blacks, and some of them are decent people. But black people are very different from white people. Perhaps the difference has something to do with inherent racial characteristics; perhaps blacks are, on the whole, not quite as intelligent or as rational as whites. Perhaps it has something to with their cultural background, the fact that they come from a backward civilization. I admit that the negro slaves were oppressed. But in any case, *white people should not mix with blacks.*' The speaker has carefully avoided saying that blacks are 'bad'; but he has made a value-judgment: whites should not mix with blacks. And if you ask him why they should not, he will probably give you this kind of answer: 'In our part of the world, where you find blacks, you find crime. The black people I know are, as a general rule, not well educated. Many of them are on public welfare. The white liberals who keep telling us how nice blacks are still know enough not to walk through the black neighbourhoods at night or send their children to schools in black areas. The black people have different cultural roots than we do. Other oppressed minorities have worked hard to rise up from poverty. But the black leaders keep running to the government for more and more public welfare aid.'

A tolerant man can agree with most of what the bigot has just said. There *is* crime in black ghettos. Many blacks *are* on welfare. Black people *do* have different cultural roots than white people have. How can the tolerant man persude the bigot that it does not *follow* that blacks are people that we should not make an effort to 'mix with'? He can feed the bigot utilitarian or deontological arguments. He can try to show him that integration may help to promote the general happiness. But as we have seen, the bigot may not accept his critic's ethical *standard*. He may not, for example, be a utilitarian. And even if he is, he can produce utilitarian arguments of his own and conclude, 'In the abstract, racial integration is a noble ideal to strive for; but given the circumstances – the crime, the deep-rooted hostility, etc. – we should give up these blind hopes for successful mixing of the races.' In giving utilitarian arguments, the bigot may simply be rationalizing his prejudice, but we cannot afford to pre-judge his motives.

Here is an alternative strategy of response. We can invite the bigot to consider whether he has considered *all* facts *relevant* to his judgment. We can argue that while all his premises are true or reasonable, his data are incomplete. Consider this analogy from the law. When a witness is sworn in at a trial, he is directed to tell the truth, the whole truth, and nothing but the truth. He is not only directed to refrain from giving false information; he is also directed to give all relevant true information, the 'whole' truth. This demand is more complex than many jurists have recognized; it is not easy for the average witness to know exactly what information is relevant to the issue at hand. Most witnesses are honest when they tell us, 'I did not realize at the time of the trial that such-and-such information was important.' Every witness knows something about the law, but few witnesses are authorities on the law. And while the bigot knows something about blacks, he is clearly not an authority on blacks. So while our 'intelligent' bigot knows a few facts about blacks, he is ignorant of a good many others, and he is also ignorant of some that may well be *relevant* to the kind of judgment that he is making, namely, that blacks are people that we should not make an effort to mix with.

Is the bigot aware of the fact that in communities A, B, and C integration appears to have been successful? Has the bigot weighed the fact that for many years blacks have been denied many learning opportunities open to whites? Does the bigot know anything about the African cultural heritage? Has he paid proper attention to the European tradition of militancy, exploitation, and persecution? If the bigot has pre-judged in this kind of situation, it is because he has judged in ignorance in two ways; he is not aware of certain relevant facts, and he is not aware that these facts are relevant. He has made his judgment *prior to* taking into account (a) particular facts and (b) what kind of facts may be relevant to the judgment.

When faced with this challenge, the bigot has three alternative responses open to him: he can withdraw or suspend his judgment; he can insist that he has weighed all the relevant data; or he can argue that no new data can possibly outweigh the data on which he has based his judgment. If he withdraws or suspends his judgment, he no longer poses a problem. Say that he insists that he has weighed all the relevant data. There is room for discussion here. We can test him by raising specific points. We may get him to admit that he has not considered this or that particular fact. If he keeps insisting that the points we are bringing up are not relevant to his judgment, or are trivial, we can try to show him why they are both relevant and important. If he is still unimpressed, it may well be that there is no value in continuing to try to change his mind. He may be irrational, incapable of understanding reasons. Or he may have a value-system that is extremely different from ours. Again, if he argues that no new data can *possibly* outweigh the data on which he based his original judgment, we can test him by raising specific points. We can try to show him that he is not being consistent, that he is not being honest with himself, or that he is not clear about his own hierarchy of values. If we fail, it may be because we have not been able to bring the key facts to his attention. Or it may again be because he is irrational, or because his value-system is genuinely and profoundly different from ours.

If the bigot sincerely and consistently believes that the data that we have presented to him, or whatever data we shall go on to present to him, cannot outweigh his original data, we are still going to regard him as prejudiced, as having made a judgment without properly weighing all the relevant data. But we must bear in mind that a man who rejects data (as 'irrelevant' or 'insignificant') is in a different position than a man who simply ignores data. A man who ignores data is clearly ignorant; but a man who rejects data because of his basic values is only ignorant in a special sense. His value-system is warped; he lacks rudimentary moral insight. When dealing with this sort of person, there is little point in arguing about evidence, inference, and fact. We cannot change his judgments, though we can talk to him about *tolerance*, about loving one's neighbour or having reverence for life. And when even this approach fails, it is time to call in the psychotherapist.

There is much value in reminding ourselves that 'prejudice,' unlike related terms, involves conditions of judgment: warrant, justification, evidence. It has an epistemological significance that terms like 'intolerance' and 'discrimination' do not necessarily have, or have only indirectly. We have seen that prejudice involves a certain kind of pre-judgment, an unwarranted judgment about people and their real or imagined characteristics. Usually, though not always, we associate prejudice with judgments that are negative, false, and maleficent. Prejudice takes different forms and involves different kinds of ignorance. Sometimes it involves empirical errors; sometimes it involves an invalid inference from facts to values. There are times when it involves viewing a man as a member of a group, while there are other times when it does not. It involves judgment at two levels. The prejudiced man makes certain judgments about people, and he also makes certain judgments about their characteristics. Pre-judgments about their characteristics are empirical errors; pre-judgments about the people themselves are logical errors, errors in inference. The empirical errors are normally not difficult to detect or refute. The logical errors are more problematic, for often we mistake them for ordinary empirical errors, and often we are confused about how value-conclusions follow from factual premises. It is important to distinguish between the two levels of prejudice, because the form of pre-judgment dictates the appropriate strategy of response.

We all know that the primary cure for prejudice is education. But an educator has to find the appropriate educational method for dealing with each particular kind of ignorance. Many believe that direct personal experience is the best antidote to all forms of prejudice. But as we have seen, direct personal experience often breeds prejudice. There is considerable value in destroying familiar stereotypes, but here the educator is only scratching the surface of the problem. There is a need for detailed and comprehensive anthropological study at all educational levels. And since the problem or prejudice is not just a problem of inadequate empirical data but a problem of logic and values, too, we have to expect prejudice to flourish in societies that take lightly their responsibility to provide training in logic and ethics.

THE DISTINCTIVENESS OF RELIGIOUS PREJUDICE

Having considered the general concept of prejudice, we can now turn our attention to the nature of religious prejudice; and just as religion is a unique human phenomenon that cannot be explained away in terms of other phenomena, religious prejudice has certain features that distinguish it from ethnic and other forms of prejudice. Since the distinctiveness of religious prejudice has often been played down, however, I think that I should explain why it is something worth taking note of.

Let us consider a very famous theory of religious prejudice, that of Allport in *The Nature of Prejudice*. (In his later writings, Allport made certain modifications in this theory, but the version of it that we will be considering is the one that has exerted the most influence in the social sciences.) Allport is struck by what he perceives as the paradoxical role of religion: 'The role of religion is paradoxical. It makes prejudice and it unmakes prejudice. While the creeds of the geat religions are universalistic, all stressing brotherhood, the practice of these creeds is frequently divisive and brutal. The sublimity of religious ideals is offset by the horrors of persecution in the name of these same ideals. Some people say the only cure for prejudice is more religion; some say the only cure is to abolish religion. Churchgoers are more prejudiced than the average; they also are less prejudiced than the average.'[2] Allport now tries to unravel this paradox. He admits that there are certain natural and perhaps unresolvable conflicts inherent in certain aspects of religion (p. 444), but he adds that most religions have ameliorating doctrines that lessen the clash. For example, most religions teach that compassion is a virtue. So while there are irreconcilable differences between contrary sets of absolutes, there are also ways of peacefully accommodating these differences (pp. 445–6).

Unfortunately, religious issues often become a rallying point for irrelevancies that cloud realistic conflict. Prejudice, Allport argues, involves only the irrelevancies and not the realistic differences. The most basic of these irrelevancies is ethnic association. Religion stands for more than faith; it is the pivot of the cultural tradition of a group. Allport follows William James in believing that piety is often a convenient mask for prejudices that intrinsically have nothing to do with religion. James writes that 'piety is the mask, the inner force is tribal instinct.'[3] Allport puts the point this way: 'Most of what is called religious bigotry is in fact the result of a confusion between ethnocentric self-interest and religion, with the latter called upon to rationalize and justify the former' (p. 448). Allport goes as far as to suggest that it is not likely that bigotry ever is or can be exclusively religious; bigotry enters 'only when religion becomes the apologist for in-group superiority and overextends itself by disparaging out-groups for reasons that extend beyond deviation in creed' (p. 449). Allport has now set the stage for the introduction of a basic dichotomy. There are, he tells us, two kinds of religiosity; one involves an 'institutionalized' religious outlook, and the other involves an 'interiorized' one. These two outlooks are worlds apart (p. 454), and while the former is a source of religious prejudice, the latter is a safeguard against it. Some studies reveal that individuals having no religious affiliation tend to show less prejudice than church members do; but studies also show that religious training can have a positive influence on ethnic attitudes.

To unravel the paradox, we have to consider the different kinds of 'functional significance' that religion can have (p. 451). Religion has a 'crutch-like ability to bolster infantile and magical forms of thinking,' but it also supports a 'guiding and comprehensive view of life that turns the individual from his self-centredness towards genuine love for his neighbor' (pp. 451–2). The two kinds of religiosity reflect religion's two basic functions: 'Belonging to a church because it is a safe, powerful, superior in-group is likely to be linked with prejudice. Belonging to a church because its basic creed of brotherhood expresses the ideals one sincerely believes in, is associated with tolerance. Thus, the 'institutionalized' religious outlook and the 'interiorized' religious outlook have opposite effects in the personality' (pp. 452–3). Allport, of course, favours the 'interiorized,' 'universalistic' conception of religion to the 'institutionalized,' 'in-group' conception: 'It is the prevalence of ethnocentric interpretations of religion that alienates many tolerant people from the church. They turn apostate because historical religions have become overburdened with the secular prejudice of in-group safety-seekers. They judge religion not by its scriptural purity, but as it is perverted by a majority of its followers' (p. 454). Allport has here extended some general psychological theories about in-groups, out-groups, and ethnocentrism to cover religion and religious prejudice. He has argued that 'we cannot speak sensibly of the relation between religion and prejudice without specifying the sort of religion we mean and the role it plays in the personal life' (p. 456). Now, there is much to be admired in Allport's theory; but he has unwisely blurred the distinction between religious prejudice and ethnic prejudice.

Allport has tried hard to give a 'liberal' interpretation of religion. He has tried to show that there is nothing wrong with religion per se, which vitally distils ideals of brotherhood into thought and action. But in Allport's view, religion tends to become corrupted by non-religious factors, especially ethnocentric attitudes. While Allport praises religion and accepts it as 'a large factor in most people's philosophy of life' (p. 456), he admires it mainly as a means to an end, the end of promoting abstract ethical ideals. He does not say that the 'meaning' of religion is purely functional, but many of his remarks suggest that his own attitude towards religion is that of the utilitarian, the pragmatist. With his dichotomy of 'institutionalized' vs 'interiorized' religion, he implies that people are religious because they either want to feel superior to 'outsiders' or believe in a creed of brotherhood that expresses abstract ethical ideals.

Religious belief and religious life, however, are far more complex than this dichotomy suggests. The important Roman Catholic philosopher Etienne Gilson has observed that 'it is psychologically interesting to know that it does one good to *believe* there is a God; but that is not at all what the believer believes; what he actually believes is, that there *is* a God.'[4] Believing in God or the immortality of the soul is wholly compatible with both the 'interiorized' religious outlook of the philosopher and the 'institutionalized' religious outlook of the simple peasant or shopkeeper. A bigoted peasant who hates outsiders, is attracted to the security offered by membership in the in-group, and associates religion with ritual rather than morality may still genuinely believe that there is a God, that he will be saved, and so forth. And while acknowledging the very real possibility of self-deception, I suggest that it is unwise to *assume* that his religiosity *must be* purely or even primarily a matter of 'in-group safety-seeking.'

Psychologists like to uncover hidden motives. Allport does not follow Freud, who sees religion as rooted in 'totemism.' But Allport does believe that the average churchgoer either is pretending to believe things that he does not believe or is unaware of the 'real' reasons why he goes to church. Yet, the fact is that people have all sorts of reasons for being religious or going to church. William James, a more perceptive pragmatist than Allport, has explained in detail how religion is 'satisfying' in a wide variety of ways. For one thing, it is intellectually satisfying and helps to explain many things the natural sciences cannot explain. People can have philosophical reasons for being religious. People can turn to the church as a result of religious experiences and mystical insights. Before we attribute the average churchgoer's religiosity to questionable or hidden motives, we should pay serious attention to his own account of his religious commitment.[5] Though it would be a mistake to underestimate the importance of self-deception, we shall find that sometimes even the bigot can have good reasons for being a churchgoer.

By emphasizing the universalistic aspect of 'genuine' religion, Allport indirectly trivializes religious differences. He admits that there are 'realistic conflicts' in religion, and he rightly observes that such conflicts are generally divisive. But a religion is not simply a device for promoting abstract ethical ideals. Nor are religious differences always rooted in cultural or ethnic differences. People with a common cultural and ethnic background can, and often do, have *reasons* or other specifically religious motives for disagreeing with one another on matters of religious doctrine. Anabaptists have had reasons for being opposed to infant baptism; Roman Catholics can give reasons for being opposed to Pharisaic legalism and Unitarianism; Protestants can explain why they are opposed to the Catholic conception of papal infallibility. One cannot dismiss these reasons as trivial, as silly obstacles to universalism, without blurring the essential differences between religion and morality. Nor can one afford to ignore other specifically *religious* motives. Allport himself recognizes that a good many people believe that their religious beliefs are *true* and that the truth of their beliefs is independent of whatever *functions* religion has in their life.

Allport's distinction between 'institutionalized' and 'interiorized' religious outlooks itself appears to be ill-conceived. He does not explain this terminology in any detail, but his point is fairly clear: organized, ecclesiastical religion is not true religion and, if anything, tends to corrupt true religion. But being associated with a particular 'institution,' a church or denomination or community of believers, does not necessarily prevent one from being genuinely religious or loving one's neighbour; in fact, even if a person feels superior to outsiders (because, say, he thinks that he knows something important that they do not know), he is still capable of manifesting a genuine concern for them. In any case, most religious people do not think of their religious commitment, or that of their neighbour, in terms of its 'functional significance,' and any theory that overemphasizes this aspect of religion cannot do justice even to the religious bigot.

The second weakness of Allport's theory is its exaggerated account of the importance of ethnocentrism and in-group safety-seeking as psychological factors. Several considerations indicate that men are not nearly as ethnocentric as Allport would have us believe. People frequently criticize their leaders, pastors, fellow citizens, and co-religionists. People generally acknowledge that we can learn from outsiders. A popular maxim tells us that 'the grass is always greener on the other side of the fence.' People often look with reverence or nostalgia to a civilization of the past: the glory of Greece, the early church, the Renaissance, the Enlightenment. Men are often fascinated by the exotic; they enjoy travelling to faraway lands, reading about other cultures, and even attending different churches. Desire to be associated with a safe, powerful in-group is often outweighed by other values.

No student of the history of religion can fail to be impressed by the continuous formation of sects. The major religions of the modern world did not all spring up spontaneously in ancient times; most of them are rooted in an initial act of withdrawal or secession from a safe, powerful in-group. The earliest Christians were wayward Jews who consciously gave up the security of orthodoxy. The earliest Buddhists were not overwhelmed by the security offered by traditional Hinduism. The leaders of the Reformation dared to revolt against the most powerful in-group of all, the Roman Catholic church. Anabaptism, Methodism, Mormonism, and other groups came into existence because many people were not afraid to become members of an out-group. In their minds, various factors outweighed the security offered by in-group membership: scriptural purity, salvation, theological considerations, philosophical arguments, common sense, social justice, newly acquired data, and so forth. Nor will it do for a defender of Allport's theory to argue that all men who leave religious in-groups have an 'interiorized' religious outlook. It is not clear that all the Lutherans who turned away from the Catholic church were genuinely religious in a way that all the Christians who remained within the fold were not. Besides, the churches of Luther, Calvin, and the other Reformers were certainly 'institutionalized'; they did have an ecclesiastical structure. And it is not evident that the early Lutherans and Calvinists had a more 'universalistic' outlook than sixteenth-century Catholics.

No psychological theory of religious commitment is adequate which fails to take into account the importance of the desire to be 'different' as a motivating factor. Certainly people are often proud to be associated with large, powerful groups. But people are also often proud to be associated with small, exotic groups. People are also proud to be unique, to stand apart from the ordinary, conventional, and commonplace.

Being in an out-group and standing alone both have their own consolations. The satisfaction that, say, the Jews derive from maintaining certain ideals of their ancestors in the face of tremendous persecution clearly compensates for much of that persecution they suffer as members of a conspicuous out-group. Torture, threats, and bribes have all failed to convince most Jews that they should join safe, powerful in-groups.

Moreover, one's pride in being a member of a religious group is largely a function of one's having *chosen* to be or remain a member of that group. It is hard to be proud of belonging to a group one has been forced to join; and even though most of us worship in the faith of our parents and ancestors, we still in a sense choose to accept that faith. So it is not hard to understand why people choose to move from in-groups to out-groups as well as from out-groups to in-groups. Now notice that we have been thinking here in terms of choice and commitment. We now have one of the keys to understanding the distinctiveness of religious prejudice. A man does not choose to be black or handicapped or a native of Poland. But a religious commitment is an act of the will. Those who hate Jews and Catholics and Mormons know that these people have chosen to hold on to certain beliefs and ways of acting. The religious bigot sees outsiders as *wilful*.

Religion, by its very nature, transcends cultural and ethnic barriers. I am not thinking here of its value in 'distilling ideals of brotherhood into thought and conduct.' I am thinking of something more basic. What determines one's membership in a religious group? Ultimately, being a Moslem or a Methodist is a matter of *faith*. The teachings of the Bible or the Koran can be accepted by Frenchmen, Turks, Mongolians, and Ethiopians. People of all races and backgrounds can choose to model their lives after Buddha's or Jesus's. Allport is right when he says that religion can be the pivot of the cultural tradition of a group; but there are all kinds of groups, and religion is not the pivot of the cultural tradition of all of them. For example, well over nine-tenths of the citizens of France are Roman Catholics of one form or other, but we can hardly infer that France is a typically Catholic nation with a typically Catholic culture. There is an important sense in which France can be seen as a Catholic nation. But we cannot really say that Catholicism is the pivot of French culture. We need not be surprised at the fact that Jews and Protestants have held important positions in France's political, academic, and economic life.

In short, I cannot feel at ease with Allport's view that religion and culture (and even race) go hand in hand. Certainly they are related, but not as closely as Allport's theory requires them to be. Many Poles hate Germans, but if a Pole hates Germans even when they attend his Catholic church, it is certainly not because they are Catholics or because *many* Germans are Protestants. Allport's association of religious prejudice with 'irrelevancies' involving cultural and ethnic association is useful in helping us to understand a very important kind of prejudice, anti-Semitism. But anti-Semitism is a special kind of prejudice (having a religious and non-religious dimension), and it is wrong to use the same model for explaining, say, Protestant prejudice against Catholics that one uses for explaining anti-Semitism. We shall return to this point shortly.

The most serious weakness of Allport's theory is that it tries to explain religious prejudice away. Many of the things that Allport says indicate that he does not acknowledge the existence of religious prejudice:

Most apparent of all is the tendency for religious issues to become a rallying point for all sorts of irrelevancies. And whenever irrelevancies cloud realistic conflict, prejudice is in command. (p. 446)

The chief reason why religion becomes the focus of prejudice is that it usually stands for more than faith – it is the pivot of the cultural tradition of a group. However sublime the origins of a religion may be, it rapidly becomes secularized by taking over cultural functions ... When religious distinctions are made to do double duty, the grounds for prejudice are laid. For prejudice means that inept, overinclusive categories are employed in place of differentiated thinking. (p. 446).

Piety may thus be a convenient mask for prejudices which intrinsically have nothing to do with religion. (p. 447)

Abominations inevitably result when men use their religion to justify the pursuit of power, prestige, wealth, and ethnic self-interest. It is then that religion and prejudice merge. Often one can detect the fusion in ethnocentric slogans: 'Cross and Flag,' 'white, Protestant, gentile, American,' 'the chosen people,' 'Gott mit uns,' 'God's country.' (p. 447)

Nothing is easier than to twist one's conception of the teachings of religion to fit one's prejudice. (p. 447)

Catholics are less often disparaged for their faith, but inherit prejudice directed originally to immigrants, who are often poorly educated. Episcopalians are no longer persecuted for their doctrine but are sometimes disliked for being snobbish and upper-crust. Pentacostalists are considered primitive, less for their theology than for their emotionalism. Jehovah's Witnesses are persecuted for minor political deviations. In none of these cases is the prejudice primarily religious. (p. 449)

In fact, if one looks at the matter closely, it becomes doubtful whether bigotry ever is or can be exclusively religious. Differences of creed there are; realistic conflicts can occur. But bigotry enters only when religion becomes the apologist for in-group superiority and overextends itself by disparaging out-groups for reasons that extend beyond deviation in creed. (p. 449)

Allport is a careful writer who tries to avoid blanket generalizations; as an authority on prejudice, he appreciates the importance of qualifying statements with such terms and expressions as 'tendency,' 'usually,' 'may thus be,' and 'it becomes doubtful whether.' But when we reflect on the above remarks, we see that there is a central theme running through them. Allport says that prejudice means that inept categories are employed in place of differentiated thinking; the bigot confuses religious considerations with ethnic ones. But no one is more guilty of blurring this distinction than Allport, who is trying to *reduce* religious prejudice to non-religious ethnic prejudice. Though he recognizes that there are realistic conflicts in religion, differences of creed, he does not see them as having anything to do with what is called 'religious' prejudice. Prejudice, bigotry, only 'enters' when 'irrelevancies' *cloud* realistic conflict. For Allport, then, genuine religious prejudice, if it exists at all, is not very important; what *appears* to be religious prejudice is not essentially religious.

What could have led Allport to argue that religious prejudice has very little to do with religion? Here are some speculations. Allport is trying hard to give a 'liberal' interpretation of religion; he is reluctant to blame religion per se for the evils that have resulted from religious prejudice. He does not want to offend religious leaders or religious people in general. So he shifts the blame to 'irrelevancies.' And here he is not alone. How often we hear that what appears to be religious conflict in Northern Ireland, Lebanon, and the Indian subcontinent is 'really' not religious but economic, cultural, racial, social, and so on! Those who refuse to acknowledge the existence of genuine religious prejudice may think that they are friends of religion, but in reality they are people who underestimate the importance of religion in human life.

And here is a second speculation: Allport has unwisely taken anti-

Semitism as a *model* for all forms of religious prejudice. He writes: 'Most clear of all is the case of the Jews. While they are primarily a religious group, they are likewise viewed as a race, a nation, a people, a culture ...' (p. 446). Allport may have forgotten that the Jews are a very special case. As a general rule, they have not made fine distinctions between their culture, religion, and life-style; the Jews are, above all, a people. So anti-Jewish prejudice is a special case, not the 'most clear of all.' It is dangerous to draw an analogy between hostility to Jews and hostility to, say, Italian Catholic immigrants. A white, Anglo-Saxon Protestant living in Toronto or New York can have an irrational hostility to all Catholics, whether or not they are poor, uneducated, or unaccustomed to speaking English. It is Allport, not the bigot, who has trouble distinguishing between the bigot's hostility to Catholics and his hostility to uneducated immigrants. I suspect, then, that Allport has used anti-Semitism as a paradigm of religious intolerance and has generalized from it to Protestant anti-Catholicism, hostility of Christians to Moslems, and so forth. Unlike Allport, most of us can distinguish between the religious prejudice of theological anti-Semites and the racist prejudice of Nazi propagandists (though we can also see how the latter incorporates, and indeed is rooted in, the former).

If a person believes that 'all Jews are obsessed with money,' he is clearly prejudiced, for as Allport rightly points out, the bigot does not have good reasons for believing that all Jews are obsessed with money. This case may well be one of ethnic prejudice, but we cannot be sure; this particular bigot may associate love of money with 'the teachings of the rabbis.' In any case, we do not have to look hard for examples of genuine religious prejudice. Consider these pre-judgments: 'Jews should suffer because they killed the Messiah.' 'Jews are dangerous because they believe in ritual sacrifice of young Christian boys and desecration of Christian holy objects.' 'Roman Catholics are anti-democratic.' 'Mormons try to promote promiscuity.' These are all hasty judgments that rest on the flimsiest of evidence; yet, men have been vilified on the basis of this flimsy evidence. The prejudice here is not ethnic, economic, or social; it is religious. The bigot has made his judgment before considering the following important questions: 'Is the account of the death of Jesus that we find in the New Testament wholly reliable? Can a man be held responsible for the mistakes of his distant ancestors? Is there much empirical data to support the contention that Jews perform ritual sacrifice of Christians? Are not many Catholics social reformers, good citizens, people who live at peace with their non-Catholic neighbours?

Do the holy works of Judaism actually teach that it is proper to desecrate the holy objects of other men? Is there anything in Mormon teaching that justifies promiscuity?' Because he has not asked himself questions like these, the bigot has ended up with an unwarranted judgment; he has failed to understand the *religious views and practices* of his neighbours.

You may feel that we have spent too much time looking at the weaknesses of Allport's theory, even if it has been very influential in the psychological study of prejudice and intolerance. But if Allport is right, and there are many people who think along the same lines as he does, then there is little point in undertaking an inquiry into the nature of religious prejudice and intolerance. If my arguments against Allport's position have been fair, then we must conclude that religious prejudice is a distinctive form of prejudice that has certain aspects which cannot be explained by a general theory of prejudice. I hope that I have established at least this much: since religion is significantly different from race, colour, national origin, and other human 'characteristics,' religious prejudice must pose problems that are not posed by other forms of prejudice.

This fact has practical implications. If religious prejudice is a mysterious, deep-rooted psychological difficulty, then the cure for the disease is psychotherapy; if religious prejudice is founded on ignorance, then the appropriate response to it is education. If religious bigots really understood the religion of their neighbours, then 'in-groups' and 'out-groups' would not matter very much to them. Education usually – though not always – can bring people to such an understanding. It is obviously easier to deal with ignorance than with pathological insecurity. This fact should serve as an incentive to us to strive to show bigots that Jews and Catholics and Moslems and Mormons do not hold all the pernicious views that have been attributed to them. And while our society should not ignore the insights of Kierkegaard, Marx, Freud, and others concerning hidden human motivation and self-deception, we should not let any psychologist convince us that prejudice necessarily has such latent roots that it can only be combatted by a psychotherapist.

We also must recognize that prejudices have a way of becoming incorporated into religious creeds and outlooks. Allport has described one mechanism by which this incorporation comes about: religious issues often become a rallying point for irrelevancies, ethnic and otherwise. There are other mechanisms. A clergyman may have cold utilitarian reasons for trying to convince his flock that outsiders are evil men who are doomed to perdition; such warnings, for that is what they amount to, tend to encourage unreflective men to remain pious insiders. Here it is religious commitment, not nationality or ethnic background, that *defines* the 'in-group' and the 'out-group.' And very often a fanatic religious leader's powers of perception have been so warped by his theological presuppositions that he simply cannot understand the beliefs and actions of outsiders. When the medieval popes persecuted Jews, it was not simply because they were seeking security but at least partly because their peculiar interpretations of the New Testament and their total ignorance of the true foundations of Judaism led them to think the most outrageous things about Jews. In any case, we must not follow Allport in setting up an artificial wall between prejudice and realistic conflict; prejudice is, regrettably, a real and important aspect of most religious creeds and outlooks.

It is often said that people need scapegoats, 'outsiders' on whom they can blame their personal problems, men that they can look down on and feel superior to. Whether or not people actually *need* scapegoats, most people certainly manage to find them. We have a right to expect a theory of religious prejudice and intolerance to supply us with more than just this simple, obvious fact. We have a right to expect it to provide us with a thorough and plausible explanation, in great detail, of how the noblest dimension of human experience became a prolific source of misery and evil.

3

Tolerance without relativism

In a preliminary note, I explained why I believe that one does not have to be a relativist to be tolerant; and I went even further, arguing that relativism is not even compatible with the spirit of tolerance. But the view that being tolerant requires one to be a relativist is so widespread and so pernicious that I feel obliged to add to my preliminary remarks about it.

I have described a 'relativist' as someone who believes that something important that is generally regarded as absolute or objective is actually dependent on the background, character, or attitudes of particular individuals or societies. I am not altogether satisfied with this definition and am well aware that textbooks of social science and philosophy offer dozens of alternative definitions; it appears that almost all social scientists and philosophers recognize that there is a 'problem of relativism,' but no one is completely clear about what the problem is.

We saw earlier that at the core of religion lie some very important things: metaphysical beliefs (beliefs about the ultimate nature of reality) and ethical commitments (views about basic ways of acting or behaving). Such metaphysical beliefs as 'God exists,' 'God is one,' 'God is omniscient,' and 'The soul survives the death of the body' make up part of a man's religious *creed*. The rest of his creed is made up of certain beliefs about history (for instance, 'God led the Jews out of Egypt,' 'Jesus was crucified'). Being religious also involves having certain ethical commitments ('One should love his neighbour,' 'One should not commit adultery'), and these commitments lead a man to live a particular religious *way of life*. Most religious men think that their metaphysical beliefs and ethical judgments are, if not true, at least more reasonable than the alternatives.

According to the religious relativist, these men are dogmatic, and their dogmatism inevitably leads to bigotry and intolerance. He argues that the most fundamental religious beliefs cannot be known to be true or false in any objective sense. Often he goes a step further by arguing that the most fundamental religious beliefs cannot even be known to be substantially more reasonable or plausible than the principal alternative religious beliefs. He promises us that if we accept his point of view we shall be freed from our intolerance and narrowness of mind; and sometimes he also warns us that unless we join him in spreading the gospel of religious relativism we shall have to share the blame for the continuing hostility among men of different religious commitments.

The limited scope of our inquiry prevents us from giving relativistic theories the careful attention they deserve. But let us consider some aspects of relativism that have been seen as relevant to the problem of religious intolerance.

POPULAR RELIGIOUS RELATIVISM

Before we consider the views of some relativist philosophers, let us look at the kind of religious relativism that one encounters in dealing with simple men, non-intellectuals, ordinary believers. Many men do not believe in the possibility of religious or metaphysical knowledge. Few non-philosophers believe that the existence or non-existence of God can be proved by means of philosophical or empirical arguments, and even those who believe that the words of the Bible or some other sacred work are true will be quick to point out that their religious beliefs are *articles of faith*. When they talk about their 'faith,' they are usually telling us that they do not believe that one can show religious beliefs to be true or false in the way that he can show ordinary empirical beliefs to be true or false. They are telling us that to hold a religious belief is to have made a decision rather than a discovery. They are not saying that they have no reasons for believing what they believe about God and freedom and the soul; but they are saying that their reasons do not give them *knowledge*, only *grounds for believing*.

Many of the religious people I have known have described religious commitment in this sort of way: 'We cannot know in this life whether or not God exists. Perhaps we shall be able to know at some time in the future; but we cannot know now. Still, we must decide whether or not to believe in a personal God. This decision is one of the most important that a man has to make, and the decision that he makes influences the whole course of his life. "Agnosticism" will not do; it is a dishonest position, for most people who profess to be "agnostics" act like atheists and in their heart of hearts *are* atheists. The existence or non-existence of a personal God is too important a subject on which to suspend judgment; one's religious views (or anti-religious views) shape thought and action in a way and to a degree that most other views do not. The alternatives before us are fairly clear. As children we had little or no choice in religious matters and accepted uncritically whatever our parents and teachers told us. Now that we are mature, rational, responsible human beings, we must make our own personal commitments to positions on religious questions. Since we cannot know for sure whether or not God exists, the soul is immortal, and so forth, we must decide which alternative view it is better to hold, and we can make this decision by evaluating each of the alternative views in terms of certain criteria of what it is good to believe. If belief in God brings *peace of mind* or is an *incentive to morality* or gives one *the feeling that life is meaningful*, it is a good belief to hold. If a belief is emotionally satisfying and intellectually satisfying, then even though we cannot know whether it is true or false, we have reason to believe that it is more plausible than alternative beliefs. People have the same basic values, needs, and aspirations, and that is why religious belief is so widespread.'

People who think of religious commitment in this way do not deny that one of the reasons why they are religious believers is that the existence of God and other religious beliefs *explain* certain phenomena; believing in God is one way of dealing with such mysteries as creation, infinity, and design in nature. But though they admit that religious belief can be intellectually as well as emotionally satisfying, enlightening as well as spiritually uplifting, they are reluctant to infer that such things as God's existence can be known or proved.

This conception of religious belief is relativistic because while it acknowledges that religious beliefs are important and influential, it excludes the possibility of objective religious knowledge. While the irrational fideist and the religious philosopher believe that they have found religious truth, 'seen the light,' the people that we have been considering see religious belief as an act of 'personal' commitment based on 'personal' reasons.

Let us consider some more of their testimony. If we ask Miss x, for example, why she believes in God, it is not likely that she will present us with some complex philosophical argument like Anselm's 'ontological' proof. What she will say is something like this: 'When I was a child, I was sent to a Baptist school by my parents, decent people, people I have always admired. Growing up with religious people, studying at a Baptist school, I developed a Christian vision of the universe and my place in it. Now that I have grown up, my ideas about God and the soul are more sophisticated than those I had when I was a child; but I still hold on to the basic religious ideas that I learned when I was young. I cannot conceive of a world without God, a materialistic world in which there is no order or ultimate purpose. I cannot conceive of a world without a significant beginning, a significant end, a meaning. The Christian vision of the universe seems to me to be a deeper, richer one than others that I am familiar with; and I think that it enables a person to lead a deeper, richer, more meaningful life than others do. I realize that my religious beliefs cannot be shown to be true or false, right or wrong. They represent my personal commitment, my personal way of coming to grips with the mysteries and crises of life. Since I am a reasonably charitable, agreeable, and considerate person, I think that no one has good reason to discourage me from holding the particular religious beliefs I hold. Anyway, we all have to have faith in something, and I think that most people who know me believe that my religious faith has made me a better person than I would otherwise be.' Most fanatics and philosophers are likely to regard Miss x's description of her commitment as too 'casual'; but most of us will take her at her word and will regard her account as a reasonable explanation of why she holds, and has a right to hold, the particular religious beliefs that constitute her 'faith.'

Of the various factors that have contributed to the popularity of this conception of religious belief, the one that mosts interests us is the one related to tolerance. People like Miss x are humble enough to recognize that it is not likely that most of the people who do not share their religious beliefs are simply stupid, wilful, or unenlightened. Though a Baptist, Miss x can accept the fact that her Methodist, Catholic, and Jewish friends also have their own 'personal' reasons for holding the particular religious views they hold. She may even be able to accept the fact that some of her friends have good reasons for being atheists. And while she may attempt to show all these people that Baptists have a rich, rewarding life, she will be willing to admit that her defence of Baptist Christianity is no more 'objective' than the Methodist's defence of Methodist Christianity, the Roman Catholic's defence of Catholicism, and so on. Miss x can see, for example, that her physician, Dr y, an observant Jew, is not simply a recalcitrant fool. She can see that he is capable of rational reflection on religious subjects, as are the religious teachers whose guidance he follows. She can see that her atheistic lawyer is a thoughtful, decent man too. Only philosophers and irrational fideists are arrogant enough to believe that people who do not share their religious opinions are stupid or unenlightened. Ordinary people cannot understand complex theological and metaphysical arguments; they do, however, have a natural instinct to believe things on the basis of *reasons*, and so they fall back on considerations of common sense, which are often related to values and morality.

There is something seductively attractive about the kind of relativism we have just considered, the conception of religious commitment as a 'personal,' 'subjective' thing. It certainly looks like the kind of theory that we would expect a tolerant man to hold; after all, if religious commitments are purely 'personal' things, then it is as foolish to be critical of another person's faith as it is to be critical of the way he wears his hair or the brand of tobacco that he smokes. But can we really accept this view of religious belief? Though it leaves a place open for reason, it runs perilously close to irrationalism. If you challenge Mr w to explain why he holds the particular religious beliefs he holds, he can give you the blunt answer, 'Because I find these beliefs satisfying.' Who can argue with him? Even if one does not like the reasons he gives for finding them satisfying (for instance, they give him peace of mind, or they make him feel less alienated from his environment), one cannot deny that he finds those beliefs satisfying. One might argue that he would find other beliefs more satisfying and that if he does not consider these alternative beliefs, he is being irrational after all. But then he could respond that as reasons for holding religious beliefs are rather personal things, we should not browbeat him. We may want to criticize Mr w for being an intellectual coward, someone who refuses to evaluate specific arguments and hides behind the view that traditional philosophical and theological inquiry is futile. Still, as much as we challenge him on this point, we cannot explain away the fact that philosophical and theological arguments have rarely if ever been absolutely conclusive. We can all see that philosophers and theologians have agreed on few things, at least where religious belief is concerned, and that it is extremely difficult to turn back the view that philosophical and religious commitments are essentially matters of 'opinion.'

There is a fruitful line of response to popular religious relativism, one which focuses on the nature of 'personal' reasons. The concept of a 'personal' reason is central to the theory, and the first question we should ask a proponent of the theory is when (if ever) desires, emotions, and feelings count as (good) reasons. Consider these exchanges:

(a) TEACHER
Why did you steal your class-mate's pet turtle?
STUDENT
Because I wanted to.
TEACHER
That's not a very informative answer. It's quite obvious that you wanted to. But I want to know why you did something that you know is wrong.
STUDENT
Because I felt like doing it.

(b) PROSECUTOR
And so you killed your wife because you found her in bed with the milkman?
DEFENDANT
Yes. I was swept away by my emotions. I was furious, irrational. I didn't realize what I was doing.

(c) Y: How could you do something so terrible to your friend? Z: I had my reasons. Y: What were your reasons? Z: I can't say; they're personal.

In the first exchange, the teacher is trying to show the child that he did not have any good reasons for stealing his class-mate's property. She knows that in some sense the boy *wanted* to steal the turtle and *felt* like stealing it. The boy's act was obviously not unmotivated, uncaused; but in stealing the turtle he was not being rational. For the teacher, the answers 'I wanted to' and 'I felt like doing it' are not informative. At best they are bad reasons; and it is possible that they are not reasons at all. In exchange (b), the defendant is telling us that it was not reason but emotion that led him to murder his wife. He does not consider his fury a *reason*; rather, his fury was something that prevented him from being rational. He did not even realize what he was doing. And in (c), it is not cler that z actually did have reasons for harming his friend. It may be that z is simply too embarrassed to admit to y that he had no (good) reasons for doing what he did. Perhaps he too acted on the basis of emotion rather than reflection and is simply hiding behind the nebulous excuse that his 'reasons' were 'personal.' After all, z knows that y has no access to z's 'personal reasons.'

Now, I am not going to offer a theory of how reasons differ from causes and motives; but I think we should draw our relativist friend's attention to the fact that even though the concept of reason is not more sharply defined than most of our concepts, it is not wholly up to the individual to determine what counts as a 'good' or 'acceptable' reason or even what counts as a *reason*. In the various situations of everyday life, people have become accustomed to expecting certain kinds of responses when they inquire after one's reasons for having believed or done something. The responses of the relativist are usually given in terms of desires, emotions, and feelings, and he considers these responses adequate. But many people find these responses evasive and insincere. Religious beliefs, after all, do exert a great influence on one's behaviour and hence on the lives of those with whom one comes into contact. Heliogabulus and Hitler wanted to believe what they believed and felt like doing what they did. They may well have thought that they had good reasons for their beliefs and actions. Yet, we would not have thought them rational if they simply told us that they had personal reasons. Holding religious beliefs is ordinarily quite different from holding the kind of beliefs Heliogabulus held. Religious beliefs and the actions they give rise to are far from unimportant. The religious relativist often admits that they are important; but we have to wonder whether he really appreciates how very important they are.

It is worth considering why the religious relativist considers his reasons 'personal' in a way that most reasons are not. He could argue that these reasons cannot be articulated; but then many will wonder whether he has any reasons at all. There are cases, as in exchange (c), where one may want to pretend that he has reasons (so as not to appear irrational, stupid, callous, and so forth). To say that one has reasons that cannot be articulated is to invite the suspicion that he does not have genuine reasons but only desires, emotions, and feelings. One could argue, however, that the reasons are personal because they are based on a value-judgment, one that is in turn rooted in his particular temperament. He could insist that it is futile to argue about religious beliefs with a man who does not evaluate beliefs by the particular pragmatic criterion that he himself employs. Here, though, we find him presupposing that pragmatic evaluations are themselves purely subjective and incapable of being questioned. It is possible to criticize a pragmatic criterion or any other basic value.

If Mr w defends his religious beliefs by arguing that he finds them 'satisfying,' we can offer various rational arguments to show him that being satisfied may not be the only important thing in life. Our Aristotelian or Kantian arguments may not convince Mr w to alter his religious beliefs; but perhaps he has an obligation to consider these arguments. Perhaps he also has an obligation to consider those metaphysical arguments that he has rather casually dismissed as being wholly irrelevant to matters of religious commitment. One can even argue that Mr w has not applied his own criterion properly, that is, that even though he may find his present religious beliefs 'satisfying,' he may find other religious beliefs (which he has not as yet even considered) even more 'satisfying.' Men know what they like, but they do not know whether they like something until they have tried it or at least given it some consideration. Besides, tastes change; the relativist can see for himself that atheists become theists and vice versa.

The religious relativist may be faced with a dilemma. If he argues that his 'personal' reasons cannot be articulated, he leaves himself open to the objection that his beliefs may be irrational, based on desires, emotions, and feelings. Perhaps he is simply deceiving himself in believing that he is being rational about religious matters. However, when he specifies his informal criteria for choosing religious beliefs and describes how he has arrived at his own particular beliefs, he is bringing out into the open criteria and procedures that are, though in one sense 'personal,' vulnerable to critical analysis. If he refuses to defend his values and criteria, he can no longer talk casually about rationality and good reasons; he has retreated into dogmatism and irrationality. But if he makes the effort to defend his criteria and beliefs, he is no longer taking advantage of his view that his reasons are *personal*. Challenging his criteria is not the same as directly challenging his religious beliefs; but it does amount to challenging his right to hold those beliefs. If Mr z defends his religious beliefs on the grounds that they make him a morally better person, then in challenging his criterion, or his assumption that his religious beliefs make him a better person, we are not showing that his religious beliefs are *false*. But we have played the game according to his rules, and one of his key rules is that truth and falsity are irrelevant here.

Are the reasons one encounters in books of philosophy and theology and apologetics really all that 'impersonal'? Philosophers from Plato to Bergson have suggested that the metaphysical apprehension or ultimate reality involves a kind of intuition. The gap between the intellectual's reasons and Mr w's reasons may not be as great as Mr w has assumed. What is a matter of intuition to one man, of course, is a matter of mere opinion to another. Still, there is clearly an element of dishonesty involved in hiding behind the claim that one's reasons are 'personal.' Most philosophers and theologians and apologists have had the courage of their convictions and have been willing to defend reasons and arguments they have made explicit. If the religious relativist is not prepared to do the same, it is not because philosophers and theologians and apologists rarely agree with one another, but because he is significantly less rational than these men.

Miss x is to be commended for recognizing that her own religious commitment is based largely on the way in which she was brought up. She is also to be commended for liking and associating with decent people who do not happen to share her religious views. Most of us are not so deterministic, so fatalistic, that we cannot see ourselves abandoning beliefs and values that were imposed on us as children. We have an obligation to ask ourselves whether the beliefs we hold are truly as reasonable as the alternative beliefs. The teachings of Judaism and Christianity, Buddhism and Islam, Catholicism and Methodism, are, though significantly similar in many areas, far from identical. If religious creeds are worth taking seriously, then the differences between one creed and another are worth taking seriously.

Religious relativists usually assume that what 'really matters' in religion is its ethical content. I pictured Miss x as arguing, 'Since I am a reasonably charitable, agreeable, and considerate person, I think that no one has good reason to discourage me from holding the particular religious beliefs I hold.' Many religious relativists appear to believe that any religion that makes a man a *better* person is a true religion. But while ethical prescriptions constitute an important part of religion, it is wrong to identify religion with morality. Religion and morality are only identical if one strips away the metaphysical, ritual, and other dimensions of religion. The religious relativist may be right in believing that these other dimensions of religion are not as important as the ethical dimension. But we have to wonder if he understands the nature of religion as a unique form of human experience. He is certainly not going to have an easy time selling religious tolerance if he tries to do it by convincing pious men that the non-ethical dimensions of religion are silly or trivial. It will be easier for him to sell it by simply directing their attention to ethical principles embodied in their religion; but to do this does not require one to be a relativist. In any event, it is certainly not obvious that the non-ethical dimensions of religion, that is, the dimensions of religion other than the ethical one, are insignificant or even secondary. The creedal and mystical may be as important as the ethical.[1] If it is even *possible* that there is a God, that God led the Israelites out of the house of slavery, that the son of God died on the cross for the sins of man, are not such possibilities worthy of our most respectful attention?

METAPHYSICAL RELATIVISM

Philosophers have defended and attacked all kinds of relativistic theories. The greatest of the ancient Sophists, Protagoras of Abdera, advanced and defended a radical form of epistemological, metaphysical, and ethical relativism, and the first great philosophers, Socrates and Plato and Aristotle, were quick to recognize the importance, complexity, and dangerousness of his doctrine. Some of the greatest philosophers have entertained relativistic ideas – Nietzsche is one who immediately comes to mind – and many important thinkers of our century have continued the tradition. Indeed, relativism has never been more popular than it is today, and its popularity has been increasing. Many books and articles have been written about relativism, and I am realistic enough to realize that whatever I say about it will fall very short of being definitive.[2]

Philosophical relativism appears in a variety of guises, as subjectivism, idealism, historicism, humanistic pragmatism, and so on. Since we are concerned with relativism in its relation to religion, we shall focus our attention on theories that see metaphysical or ethical beliefs as 'relative' to particular individuals or societies, and we shall start by looking at metaphysical relativism.[3]

Let us consider the two things that appear to bother almost all advocates of this doctrine. First, metaphysical beliefs appear to be 'subjective' in a way that ordinary empirical beliefs are not. For over two thousand years philosophers and religious leaders have tried to prove that certain metaphysical beliefs are true; they have tried to show that they possess a metaphysical knowledge that is not shared by those who hold different metaphysical beliefs. When we turn to the history of philosophy and theology, we find a battleground of warring sects, with theists against atheists, idealists against materialists, Unitarians against Trinitarians, and so on; and while most metaphysical and religious believers are convinced of being in possession of some 'ultimate truth,' no one has yet been able to produce the 'ultimate verification,' the proof to end all metaphysical and theological debate. (Some men think that they have found the ultimate verification, too, but they have had a very hard time getting others to agree that they have. If a metaphysical or theological argument fails to impress the great majority of reasonable men, is this failure not more likely a reflection of the limitations of the argument than of the limitations of the people that it has failed to impress?) The metaphysical relativist is highly sensitive to the fact of the traditional and continuing multiplicity of conflicting metaphysical and theological opinions. He does not have much confidence in metaphysical arguments; he tends to see them as artificial and question-begging. And he is not intimidated by the fideist's claim to know about the ultimate nature of reality; for he can see that fideists disagree, and which (if any) should he trust? But the metaphysical relativist is not only impressed by the fact that there is widespread *disagreement* on metaphysical and theological subjects; he knows that this disagreement does not in itself prove that metaphysical beliefs are 'subjective.' Two other factors have played a role in his arriving at this conclusion.

One factor is his belief that every metaphysical argument that he has come across is inadequate. The second is his speculation about the 'real' significance of metaphysical beliefs. Why, he wonders, must we accept the conventional opinion that the value of philosophical and religious teaching lies in the objective truth of the pronouncements it embodies? For if a metaphysical idea is subjective, hypothetical, or culture-bound, it is still as capable of influencing men as it would be if it were objectively and eternally true. Armed with this insight, he goes out to find the 'real value' of metaphysics and religion, and he rarely comes back disappointed. Then he tells us about his 'discovery': metaphysical and theological beliefs are absolute presuppositions of natural science or rules for interpreting experience or meaningless expressions of a neurosis; their 'real function' is to make us happier or more aggressively moral or capable of carrying on the process of scientific inquiry. The irony here is that the metaphysical relativist is not impressed by the fact that most reasonable men disagree with him on this point. As he sees things, they are 'dogmatic' while he is 'enlightened.'

Belief in the subjectivity of metaphysical ideas is the epistemological impetus to adopting the position of metaphysical relativism. Of course, besides this impetus, there is a moral one, the desire to construct a theory that will promote or justify tolerance. F.C.S. Schiller, a humanistic pragmatist, has written that 'a practical recognition of Relativity' has become 'a matter of urbanity and manners, and only a bigot or a pedant can ignore it.' 'Any unity Philosophy can aim at will have to be of a very tolerant and elastic kind, and such that it can find room for personal differences, without crumbling'; we must discredit 'all philosophical methods which are dogmatic, authoritarian, and intolerant, and favour those which are freer and more flexible, and afford ample scope for individual differences and personal preferences ...'; we must make 'allowance for age, sex, circumstances, and point of view. We have learned, though slowly and with difficulty, the necessity of toleration. We have learned, that in the most stubborn cases, we can agree to differ.'[4]

The German historicist Wilhelm Dilthey has argued that the historical consciousness of the relativity of every kind of faith is 'the last step towards the liberation of man,' and that through it 'the mind becomes sovereign over the cobwebs of dogmatic thought.'[5] William James, humanistic pragmatist and psychologist of religion, has repudiated the dogmatism of scholastic orthodoxy and empiricism alike: 'The greatest empiricists among us are only empiricists on reflection: when left to their instincts, they dogmatize like infallible popes. When the Cliffords tell us how sinful it is to be Christians on such "insufficient evidence," insufficiency is really the last thing they have in mind. For them the evidence is absolutely sufficient, only it makes the other way.' We must treat dogmatic absolutism, James tells us, as 'a weakness of our nature from which we must free ourselves.'[6]

It is not clear which impetus to adopting metaphysical relativism comes first, the epistemological or the moral one; I suspect that this varies from relativist to relativist. But these two factors, belief in the subjectivity of metaphysical and theological ideas and hostility to dogmatism and intolerance, are almost always at the heart of the metaphysical relativist's position.

People have rejected metaphysical relativism for a variety of reasons. The positivists reject it because they see it as giving metaphysical beliefs an undeserved place in our world-view. Fideists and other religious believers who see certain sacred works as providing us with metaphysical knowledge are apt to agree with Cardinal Garrone's assessment of relativism:

Certainly there is no difficulty in admitting a healthy philosophical pluralism, due to the diversity of regions, cultures, and mentalities through which different ways to the same truth can be pursued ... However, it is not possible to admit a philosophical pluralism which compromises the fundamental nucleus of affirmations connected with revelation, since a contradiction is not possible between the naturally knowable truths of philosophy and the supernatural truths of faith. With this in view, one can then affirm that the very nature of the Judeo-Christian revelation is absolutely incompatible with all relativism epistemological, moral or metaphysical ...[7]

The most common criticism of metaphysical relativism, however, is that it fails to recognize that proponents of some metaphysical position have 'conclusively established' the objective truth, or at least the great reasonableness, of that particular position.

Given the metaphysical relativist's view of things, none of these criticisms is likely to bother him very much. But his position is also open to psychological or pragmatic criticisms, and these may well touch a nerve. It can be argued that if metaphysical relativism were to become the most popular theory of the nature of metaphysical beliefs, people would no longer be able to take their own metaphysical beliefs seriously; and since moral judgments are influenced by metaphysical beliefs, metaphysical relativism could also contribute to the rise of an unhealthy ethical relativism. If you break down a man's belief in divine justice, human freedom, and a spiritual realm, you may lead him to abandon his most basic ethical principles. Also, metaphysical relativism is likely to lead a man to do too much tolerating; it would seem to promote moral weakness, apathy, and passivity rather than genuine tolerance, tolerance of what ought to be tolerated. To commit oneself to a thoroughgoing relativism may well be to commit oneself to accepting behaviour that intuitively seems terribly immoral; in our time we have seen how tyrants often support their cause with complex metaphysical theories about human nature, human destiny, and so forth.

A more general psychological-pragmatic criticism is that the human mind needs and seeks absolutes, and any philosophy that does not offer any is apt to be unattractive to all but a handful of men. Thus, while he is not very happy about it, the historicist relativist Benedetto Croce admits that 'there is a widespread recurrence of the longing for eternal truth, for a truth not to be discussed or corrected or modified, a constant rule of life for humanity, a sure guide to the haven where it would be. And since the Church of Rome offers such a rule and such guidance more generously than any other existing institution, it is on the need for an eternal truth that it most effectively bases the appeal to take shelter under its wings.'[8] What the metaphysical relativist has to offer, a theory about the nature of metaphysical beliefs, cannot *replace* what metaphysical absolutists give us, specific theories about the ultimate nature of reality; and the human condition being what it is, other men will have to do what the metaphysical relativist is reluctant or unable to do.

We have seen Cardinal Garrone distinguish between a 'healthy' philosophical pluralism and a relativistic one. For Garrone, a 'healthy' pluralism is one that does not compromise 'the fundamental nucleus of affirmations connected with revelation.' Perhaps there are other ways of distinguishing between a 'healthy' pluralism and a relativistic one. Croce, while arguing that 'a definitive pronouncement of total truth would mean the burial of thought,' also suggests that man 'could not think if he did not already live in truth, in the light of God.'[9] The English historicist R.G. Collingwood has argued that metaphysical 'presuppositions' are neither true nor false, but he has also pointed out that certain metaphysical 'presuppositions' have been made *semper, ubique, ab omnibus*, except by certain barbarians who would have brought about the collapse of science and civilization.[10] Schiller, recognizing a significant uniformity in human needs and wants, reminds us that 'the personal philosophies which alone seem to have any logical warrant, will necessarily differ. But it does not follow that they will differ without limit and without measure, and will not allow themselves to be classified in any way.'[11]

Certain philosophers who are widely regarded as metaphysical relativists, then, have recognized that there are certain attributes and attitudes common to all 'civilized' men, and some have even suggested that there is some vague, general 'perennial philosophy,' one that is in no way complete but modified by individual and cultural differences. When they talk in this way, historicists and humanistic pragmatists are pluralists but not relativists. Moreover, in spite of their cynicism with regard to metaphysical proofs, arguments, and reasons, many philosophers commonly associated with the doctrine of metaphysical relativism would admit, when pressed, that some metaphysical theories are 'better' than others. The metaphysical theories of Plato and Spinoza, of Jews and Christians, are still taken very seriously, even by critics, in a way that most metaphysical theories of the past are not. These famous theories are not only interesting or exciting or colourful; they have a certain plausibility and profundity too. And one reason that they have this plausibility and do not seem wholly silly and extravagant is that they can be, and indeed have been, supported by various sorts of rational defence. Also, we should not overestimate the amount of rivalry that exists among metaphysical theories; insights of one philosophy or religion are often absorbed into new philosophies and religions. For example, many Jewish ideas have been incorporated into Christianity and Islam; and many of Plato's ethical ideas have been incorporated into Aristotelianism, Spinozism, and most contemporary ethical theories.

Perhaps dogmatism is unavoidable. Even the metaphysical relativist has a dogma, and sometimes he realizes that he does. There are limits to reason; reasoning requires starting-points, and not all starting-points can be derived from sense-experience. Still, as Schiller has pointed out, we have to a great extent learned the necessity of toleration, and we have learned it without having to take on a relativistic conception of the nature of our most basic and most important beliefs. Tolerance, after all, does not demand that one believe that every other person's metaphysical views are as true or as reasonable or as profound as his own. Indeed, as we saw earlier, tolerance is possible only because we are capable of putting up with things that we do not like or respect or agree with. Tolerance requires that one be prepared to sort out practical disagreements with others in a civilized way. It requires that one find ways of co-operating with men who do not share one's metaphysical outlook. It does not require that we accept a theory that will lead to the kind of paralysing scepticism and lack of commitment that a pure relativism inevitably breeds. The metaphysical relativist's 'cure' for intolerance is not only ineffective but worse than the disease.

As different as a metaphysical belief is from an ordinary empirical belief, it still has something in common with the latter which makes it very different from a poem or painting: it is a belief about reality. We may wonder whether it is possible to hold a belief about reality without believing that this belief is objectively true. The metaphysical relativist's main point is his epistemological one: it appears that we cannot know, determine, or establish that any particular metaphysical belief is objectively true. But to *hold* a belief, even as a hypothesis, speculation, or working principle, is to *believe* that something is objectively true, whether or not the belief can actually be known, determined, or established to be true. The metaphysical relativist is trying to pass off as *believing* a kind of propositional attitude, some kind of 'holding' a belief, that falls short of being genuine believing.

A final point: we must demand that the metaphysical relativist join us in a careful examination of specific metaphysical arguments. The plausibility of metaphysical relativism is dependent on the inadequacy of every possible metaphysical argument; if even one minor argument does succeed in establishing what it was intended to – that metaphysical conclusion x is substantially more reasonable than metaphysical belief not-x – then the metaphysical relativist's position has been seriously vitiated. No one has yet produced the ultimate verification for a complete religious creed or metaphysical 'system.' But it is clear that the force of the metaphysical ideas of great philosophical and sacred works is partly a function of the arguments that can be, and have been, advanced in support of these ideas; the apparent superiority of certain metaphysical arguments over others is to be taken no less lightly than the historic multiplicity of conflicting metaphysical opinions.

ETHICAL RELATIVISM

Ethical relativism also involves more than a recognition of widespread disagreement. All of us can see that different people and different societies are committed to significantly different views about how men should live; but few of us are relativists. Ethical relativism is a theory, not just a summary of certain anthropological observations.

The theory comes in a variety of styles, but here is the basic insight that underlies it:

PREMISE 1: A moral judgment (belief, value) can only be justified by another moral judgment (or other moral judgments; or other moral judgments coupled with one or more factual beliefs).

PREMISE 2: There cannot be an infinite regression of moral judgments (beliefs, values) supporting or justifying lower-order moral judgments.

PREMISE 3: There must be at least one moral judgment (belief, value), z, that is primal or fundamental.

PREMISE 4: z is rejected by some people in favour of other primal moral judgments (beliefs, values), z_1, z_2, etc.

CONCLUSION: z, z_1, z_2, et al. are 'relative,' as are all the lower-order moral judgments based on them.

In order to refute the ethical relativist's position, we have to show that a certain fundamental moral principle, z, is truer or better or more reasonable than z_1 and z_2 and all other alternative principles. But how can we defend z when we ourselves have acknowledged that it is 'primal' or 'fundamental'? At this point, even some of the most rational thinkers start talking about 'moral intuitions,' 'self-evident principles,' 'natural law,' 'the revelation from God,' 'common sense,' and so on.

Perhaps we could take all this talk about intuition and common sense seriously were it not for the data amassed by cultural relativists like

W.G. Sumner, Edward Westermarck, and Melville Herskovits. These anthropologists warn us not to be provincial, dogmatic, narrow-minded; they tell us that too many of us are 'ethnocentric' and uncritically believe that our value-system and way of life should be preferred to all others. Herskovits, for example,[12] tells us that moral evaluations are '*relative* to the cultural background out of which they arise'; having himself somehow attained a greater 'objectivity' than we non-anthropologists can ever aspire to, he goes on to explain to us how the people we call 'savages' have value-systems and ways of life which are not intrinsically inferior to our own. Unfortunately, cultural relativists like Herskovits do not realize that the theory they have attached to their empirical data has a wider application than they acknowledge. For if moral evaluations must be relative to the cultural background out of which they arise, must they not also be relative to the personal or individual background out of which they arise? Why draw the line at this mysterious level of 'culture'?[13] Why not admit that every individual interprets experience in terms of his temperament, his conceptual apparatus, his personal neuroses, and so forth? The answer here is that the cultural anthropologist thinks of the 'culture' as the single most important influence on the values and attitudes of the individual; and, at the same time, he wants to escape the charge that he is encouraging 'nihilism,' that is, an attitude towards values that will result in social instability, atrocities, and so on. But intercultural differences are no more profound than intracultural or individual ones; and if one keeps on thinking about 'primal' or 'fundamental' moral principles, one carries the cultural relativist's theory along farther than the cultural relativist wants him to; one moves in the direction of a radical ethical relativism (intracultural or personal relativism) that is for all intents and purposes a form of nihilism.

We have many good reasons for concluding that cultural relativists have overestimated the importance of enculturation and ethnocentrism. There is widespread disagreement about how to live *within* cultures. Cultures are not static; they are born, die, and undergo radical transformations. Every society contains groups of men who have tenaciously refused to accept the values of the society's leaders. Charismatic reformers have been able to induce even weak people to transcend the way in which they were brought up. Many people are convinced that the values and way of life of their society are significantly inferior to those of other societies. We all belong to more than one community – a political one, racial one, religious one, linguistic one, family one, professional one, etc. – and so we have been exposed to conflicting values and views about how to live. (Three French Canadians may perceive themselves respectively as being, above all else, French-speaking, Canadian, and Roman Catholic.) Intercultural dialogue is not only possible but often useful; sometimes it leads us to change our mind about the morality of some basic institution. At least some of our moral judgments are determined more by rational considerations than by the way in which we were brought up. I could list at least another ten reasons why the cultural relativist's position is untenable, but I think that I have given enough to show that moral evaluations are not simply relative to the *cultural* background out of which they arise.

But having disposed of cultural relativism, we are still faced with the serious problem of what to say to the individual who does not accept our primal or fundamental moral principle(s). Take, for example, the man who is committed above *all* else to *manifesting his power*, even if doing so means murdering innocent people, torturing children and elderly people, destroying religious and educational institutions, killing himself, and so forth. We can try to convince such a person that at some level of consciousness he himself realizes that certain things take precedence over manifesting his power. But say that he will not budge an inch, that he is genuinely and deeply committed to some bizarre primal moral principle, some horrible fundamental criterion of action. If we cannot persuade him to adopt a less bizarre conception of the purpose of life, we have to take this kind of person – a Hitler, a Heliogabulus – and isolate him in such a way that he cannot do any harm. Now, if the radical ethical relativist comes along and tells us that we are dogmatic, intolerant, that we are persecuting this power-mad figure, we have to isolate him too. The fact is, though, that most of those who are radical relativists in theory are not strict relativists in reality, when confronted with the possibility of unspeakable atrocities. Most of us, relativists included, believe that there is something very wrong with a person who sincerely believes that there is nothing intrinsically bad or wrong in torturing innocent people as a means of manifesting one's power. We cannot even enter into a compromise with a man who is committed above all else to manifesting his power.

It seems that we are back to our 'intuitions.' What, after all, can we fall back on when reason is no longer relevant? But it will surely be objected that our intuitions are not always conducive to tolerance. It is one thing to isolate a Hitler or a Heliogabulus; but men have appealed to moral intuition in order to justify isolating or destroying Jews, Christians, poets, philosophers, and saints. What makes some moral intuitions better than others? What makes some primal moral principles more worthy of being tolerated than others? Why should we isolate a Hitler but not poison a Socrates?

Since pure intuitionism is as dangerous a doctrine as pure relativism (or is even perhaps a form of pure relativism), we have to find a better response to the question of how to cope with the apparent relativity of moral principles that lie beyond reason. What we need here is a theory of civilization.

Ethical relativists tend to be very suspicious about references to 'civilization' and 'civilized men,' and I often suspect that most of them would like to see these terms disappear from our language. Consider the following warning of Herskovits: 'Cultures are sometimes evaluated by the use of the designations "civilized" and "primitive." These terms have a deceptive simplicity, and attempts to document the differences implied in them have proved to be of unexpected difficulty.'[14] Many statements about the 'civilized' and the 'primitive' are, as ethical relativists have pointed out, merely expressions of biases. But the concept of civilization is not nearly as empty as ethical relativists would have us believe. 'Civilization' is not a technical term; it is a term that ordinary people occasionally use. Like all words that end in the suffix '-zation,' it refers to a certain kind of *process*. (We speak of a particular civilization or of certain civilizations, but we should not forget that the term 'civilization' primarily signifies a process that something is undergoing or has undergone.)[15] We often make judgments about the degree to which particular groups of people are or have been civilized. We say that 'savages' or 'primitive people' are relatively uncivilized, or are at an early stage in the process of civilization. We usually think that *we* are relatively advanced in the process, that is, that the groups with which we identify outselves have undergone more civilization than most other groups in history or in the contemporary world. (We can identify ourselves with various kinds of groups: ethnic, racial, political, linguistic, religious, and so forth.) People in our society tend to believe that the ancient Athenians were more civilized than the ancient Vandals, and that modern Scandinavians are more civilized than modern African tribesmen (although not necessarily in all areas of human experience).

Now, what is called 'civilization' by people in one group is sometimes dismissed as 'savagery' or 'barbarism' by people in another, For four reasons, however, I believe that assigning positions on the scale of civilization is not wholly arbitrary: 1 / We are not so ethnocentric that we cannot regard real or ideal societies or religious groups as more civilized than our own. Few people in any group regard their group as utopian. We can all see ways in which the groups with which we identify ourselves can be further civilized; and we can admire institutions and values of radically different ethnic, political, and religious groups. 2 / There appears to be some intercultural consensus with regard to the height of certain societies or religious groups on the scale of civilization. Here are some examples. Ancient Greek culture has received favourable consideration in both India and Europe. Academic scholars in various parts of the world have praised the accomplishments of the Mayan and Incan peoples. Even the barbarous Hitler has observed that 'we should not know that there was a Maya people, or should regard that fact as of no account, were it not that to the astonishment of our age the mighty ruins of the cities of such legendary peoples ever awake afresh the notice and arouse and hold the interest of researchers.'[16] 3 / There appear to be certain *trans-cultural values* that are venerated in all or most societies and religious groups. And 4 / there appear to be certain *qualities* (only indirectly related to values) that characterize any society commonly regarded as highly civilized, qualities that gradually appear as the society develops and often recede as the society disintegrates.

I owe you an explanation and defence of the last two points, both of which involve what may be called the 'conditions' of civilization. Though we are interested in a *theory* of civilization, we must recognize that these two points are essentially empirical. Consider first whether there really are trans-cultural values, abstract but basic values to be found in societies considered relatively uncivilized as well as in those considered highly civilized. It *seems to me* that there is an inexhaustible supply of historical and anthropological data which indicates that love, justice, peace, economic prosperity, wisdom, progress, self-realization, and so forth are trans-cultural values. But perhaps I have been reading the wrong history and anthropology books; or perhaps I have been reading too much *into* the *right* ones. After all, as we have seen, some very respected cultural anthropologists (and philosophers) have been ethical relativists. So I invite you to consider some of the data I have found so impressive.

1 / When we pick up an old and exotic work like the *Bhagavad Gita* or Confucius's *Lun yü*, we find in it much ethical teaching that sounds very similar to the ethical teaching of the Bible or of modern western philosophers. Consider these excerpts from the *Bhagavad Gita*: 'But to

forgo this fight for righteousness is to forgo thy duty and honour: is to fall into transgression.' 'There is no wisdom for a man without harmony, and without harmony there is no contemplation. Without contemplation there cannot be peace, and without peace can there be joy?'[17] These passages draw our attention to some very familiar values: righteousness, duty, honour, wisdom, peace, joy. Are these not the same values that Isaiah and Plato point to? Or consider these sayings of Confucius: 'Great Man is conscious only of justice; Petty Man, only of self-interest.' 'Formerly men studied for self-improvement; today men study for the sake of appearances.'[18] Have these observations lost their relevance? Still, perhaps one is being too selective if one attaches great importance to works like the *Gita* and Confucius's *Lun yü* while ignoring less famous works.

2 / After a careful study of a great deal of anthropological literature, the eminent anthropologist Clyde Kluckhohn has come to these conclusions:

The universalities in wants and the universals and near-universals in moral concepts do generate two fairly cheerful propositions:

First, the similarities in human needs and human response-potentialities across cultures do at any rate greatly heighten the possibilities of cross-cultural communication once these core likenesses have been somewhat disentangled from their cultural wrappings;

Second, while we must not glibly equate universals with absolutes, the existence of a universal certainly raises this question: If, in spite of biological variation and historical and environmental diversities, we find these congruences, is there not a presumptive likelihood that these moral principles somehow correspond to inevitabilities, given the nature of the human organism and of the human situation? They may at any rate lead us to 'conditional absolutes' or 'moving absolutes,' not in the metaphysical but in the empirical sense.[19]

3 / Even cultural relativists like Westermarck and Herskovits admit that ethical 'universals' exist. Westermarck writes, 'When we study the moral rules laid down by the customs of savage peoples we find that they in a very large measure resemble the rules of civilized nations.'[20] Herskovits recognizes the importance of 'those least common denominators to be extracted, inductively, from comprehension of the range of variation which all phenomena of the natural or cultural world manifest.'[21]

4 / If one studies Nazi documents, one finds that some of the official

aspirations of Nazi society – barbarous as it was – resemble those of our own. Consider these excerpts from the speeches of Adolf Hitler:

We wish for peace. (22 October 1933).

The great work of art bears in itself an absolute value (9 September 1937).

The government ... [is] creating and securing the conditions necessary for a really profound revival of religious life (23 March 1933).

The task which the administration of justice must set before itself is to co-operate in maintaining the life of the people and in protecting it from those elements which through their un-social tendencies either seek to escape their duties to the community or offend against the interests of the community (30 January 1937).[22]

I am not suggesting that all the values of all communities are the same; but I *am* saying that there are some abstract, basic trans-cultural values. In order to gain appeal, even Hitler and the Nazis had to be *seen* to be endorsing these values.

The question before us, then, is, given the fact that the value-systems of almost all known societies are built upon a foundation of a limited number of trans-cultural values, why is there so much ethical 'relativity,' and why are some societies more civilized than others? The answer may be that trans-cultural values are essentially *ends*, and people in different religious or political or ethnic groups disagree as to what the appropriate *means* to these ends are. Plato's *Republic*, the Bible, and the *Communist Manifesto* all deal with issues related to justice, peace, and wisdom, but they propose different approaches to these ideal ends. Perhaps height on the scale of civilization, then, is not so much a matter of what basic values are venerated by a society or religious group as it is a matter of how much or how successfully its *ideal values* have been *realized*.

If this hypothesis is true, then it is important for several reasons. First, we can see why we are not doomed to be as ethnocentric as some cultural anthropologists think we are. On reflection we realize that while our fellow citizens and co-religionists venerate (at some level of consciousness) love, justice, peace, wisdom, and so forth, they have condoned policies and institutions that conflict with these ideals. So perhaps there is nothing wrong with the *most basic* aspirations of American Protestants or African tribesmen or Chinese communists or

Turkish Moslems; and perhaps civilization is less a process of developing wholly new ideals than a process of realizing trans-cultural ones. Consider these examples. The Southern Baptist clergyman tells his flock to *love* their neighbours; yet he condones unwarranted religious discrimination. The legislator praises *peace* while voting to use force to achieve questionable economic objectives. The public accepts this inconsistency, this hypocrisy, even though it recognizes that our society or religious community would be higher on the scale of civilization if it did not condone racial intolerance and indiscriminate use of force. Perhaps the major obstacles to further civilization are confusion, cynicism, passivity, and a preoccupation with concrete personal problems.

In any case, if my hypothesis is true, then not only can we see why we are not doomed to be ethnocentric, but we can also see why rational judgments can be made about the height of other societies, even distant ones, on the scale of civilization. Barbarists may praise love, justice, peace, and wisdom, but we can see for ourselves how ineffective their methods for achieving these ends are. To some extent, the Saracens and Huns and Nazis simply disagreed with highly civilized men on questions of value; but as we have seen, the official aspirations of Nazi society to a great extent resemble those of our own. The point here is that we can make sound, rational judgments about the relative amount of civilization undergone by the ancient Athenians, the Mayans, or the Nazis because we can evaluate the *effectiveness* of the *means* that they have agreed upon for realizing trans-cultural values. If there were no trans-cultural values, then we would be left with radical ethical relativism and an empty concept of civilization. But if there are universal ethical *termini*, no matter how abstract, then as Kluckhohn has observed, intercultural dialogue on ethical questions is possible, and we can learn from people in other societies about ways of more rapidly realizing common ideals.

Of course, ethical relativists may argue here that the concepts of love, justice, and so on are as nebulous as the concepts of civilization; and they may argue that there is no satisfactory method of determining whether a particular policy or institution is an effective means of realizing a trans-cultural ideal. But we seem to be able to understand what the ancient Athenians, Hebrews, and Chinese meant when they wrote about things that sound like justice and wisdom, and we also know how to make some rational evaluations of the effectiveness of legislation, social policies, and so forth. For example, it would have been both reasonable and fair to ask a Nazi the following question: 'You claim that you wish for *peace*. Why, then, did you invade Poland?' Or this one to the Grand Inquisitor: 'You say that we should *love* our neighbour. So why are you making so many people so terribly unhappy?' The man might have had an answer, but could it have withstood the test of critical examination? Showing that x promotes or does not promote y is considerably less mysterious than showing that y ought to be promoted.

There are also three *qualities* that appear to characterize all societies that are widely regarded as advanced on the scale of civilization; these qualities, which must be distinguished from *values*, gradually appear as a society develops and often recede as it deteriorates: rationality, respect for the rights of 'outsiders,' and complexity of the value-system. 1 / If we cannot reason with people, and if they cannot reason with one another, then it is hard to regard them as civilized. As a child matures, it ordinarily becomes more rational; similarly, as a society develops, its members tend to become more rational and less emotional and superstitious. I am not making a value-judgment here; I am describing an observable phenomenon. 2 / With regard to the second quality, let me cite an observation of Westermarck: 'A stranger is in early society devoid of all rights. And the same is the case not only among savages but among nations of archaic culture as well ... When we pass from the lower races to peoples more advanced in civilization we find that the social unit has grown larger, that the nation has taken the place of the tribe, and that the circle within which the infliction of injuries is prohibited has been extended accordingly.'[23] Again, Westermarck is not making a value-judgment here but is describing an observable phenomenon. 'Primitive men' do not see those outside the 'tribe' as having the rights that those inside the tribe have. As men become civilized, they see more and more people outside the 'tribe' as having rights. In understanding why the ancient Israelites were so much more civilized than the Semitic barbarians and savages among whom they lived, it is helpful to reflect on such passages in the Pentateuch as Exodus 23:9: 'And a stranger shalt thou not oppress; for ye know the heart of a stranger, seeing ye were strangers in the land of Egypt.' 3 / Those societies and religious groups that are considered highly civilized are societies with relatively complex value-systems. The most fundamental values are trans-cultural, universal. But in advanced groups, every basic value is seen as generating or implying a wide range of secondary values.

Here, then, is a working definition of 'civilization': civilization is the process of approximating or realizing, primarily by the use of reason, the greatest possible number of trans-cultural or universal human aspirations, both for oneself and for the greatest possible number of others. Some groups are advanced in the process and others less so. One can civilize oneself, one can civilize others in one's group, and one can even civilize people outside of one's group. Whatever weaknesses it has, this working definition conforms with the way in which people in our society ordinarily use the term 'civilization.'

Does this 'theory of civilization' represent a more satisfactory response to the ethical relativist than an appeal to intuition? The confirmed ethical relativist may want to argue that there are no trans-cultural, universal ideals, or that these ideals are too nebulous to have much practical significance. I am inclined at this time to offer the following response. It is clear that human society as a whole has changed dramatically over the centuries. Individual societies have not always kept pace with human society as a whole, but with regard to any particular value, human society as a whole has moved from point *a* to point *b*. But how can we be sure that point *b* is closer to the 'ideal'? One could, after all, argue that human society is degenerating rather than improving. Many a historian looks to the glory of ancient cultures and condemns the sterility of our own. Dachau was built more than two thousand years after the Parthenon. Now, when men are *free*, they work towards realizing their aspirations; but, for reasons that we will consider in a later chapter, men often act immorally, and sometimes they even become hostile to civilization. Enemies of civilization, the people we call 'barbarists' or 'barbarians,' may argue that the transformation of human society has not been 'progressive' or that 'progress' is itself undesirable; but while they have slowed down human society's realization of its highest aspirations, they have not succeeded in *changing* the aspirations of the majority. Perhaps the things that I have called 'trans-cultural ideals' are nothing more than the aspirations of the majority of people in human society as a whole. Perhaps they are not intrinsically or absolutely superior to the desire to destroy or the desire to manifest one's power. If so, are we left in the end with a merely conventionalist ethic? Or have we come to have an insight into what is 'normal' in 'human nature'? Or have we come to understand human destiny in the context of a meaningful, purposeful universe?

In my preliminary note on relativism, I criticized proponents of a modified relativism who distinguish between great religions and not-so-great ones. Where, I asked, are we to draw the line? In my comments about civilization, I have indicated that we do have reasons for distinguishing between advanced religious communities and not-so-advanced ones. But I am not defending any form of religious relativism, modified or otherwise. For one thing, a religion is not simply a set of ideals; it involves beliefs – beliefs about reality – and contradictory beliefs cannot both be true. Also, one should not separate religions according to a simplistic dichotomy of great vs not-so-great; even when we are considering just the ethical dimension of religion, we must remember that the scale of civilization has an infinite number of points, and more than one (that is, that which separates the 'great' from the 'not-so-great') merits our consideration. There can be no question that in spite of their common ideals, different religions – even 'great' ones – occupy different positions on the scale of civilization. Finally, we must not forget that the various means of realizing trans-cultural aspirations are not equally efficient or successful.

Now, I am not suggesting here that it is always easy to determine which of two religions is higher on the scale. Such a determination involves *judgment*. One factor that makes this kind of judgment especially difficult is that there are many variables to consider; religion A may be more efficient than religion B in promoting end x (for instance, wisdom) and less efficient than B in promoting end y (for instance, peace). But we do make this kind of judgment whenever we freely and rationally choose to be Moslems rather than Christians, Presbyterians rather than Baptists, and so on.

I shall not pretend to have 'refuted' all forms of relativism in these pages; I am as wary as you are of simple 'refutations' of old and complex philosophical doctrines. What I have tried to show is that religious relativism is, for a variety of philosophical, psychological, and pragmatic reasons, a bad theory for the advocate of tolerance to make an intellectual and emotional investment in. The religious relativist, while claiming to take most religions seriously, does not take any seriously. He does not appreciate how much is at stake in religious disagreements. But religious faith involves the most powerful commitments, and if it does not appear to in our own society, perhaps that is only because most of our fellow citizens who profess to be religious are not really religious. I happen to believe that the particular religious opinions I hold are more reasonable than any others that I have been exposed to. If I did not believe this, I would give them up in favour of different ones. I shall continue to enjoy the company of men of other faiths, and I shall continue to appreciate the importance of working with them to achieve common goals. But I will not accept the relativist's view that their religious commitments are as profound as my own, if only because I cannot. And if my understanding of human nature is reasonably correct, then I can speculate with some confidence that if the religious relativist tries to make people tolerant by converting them to relativism, he will fail again and again.

4

Religious pluralism

There would be no religious intolerance in a society in which everyone held the same religious beliefs and lived the same kind of religious life; in such a society there would be nothing religious to be intolerant of. But all real societies are made up of men with different religious and philosophical outlooks. Some societies contain only very small religious minorities. Intolerance is as much a problem in these societies as in others. We obviously cannot tolerate a barbarian like Hitler or Heliogabulus who is committed to bizarre principles of action. But why are we so often unable to tolerate those members of religious or philosophical minorities who have the same basic values or aspirations that we have? One answer, as we have seen, is that we are often prejudiced, we often pre-judge people of other faiths. Another answer, as we have seen, is that we often look for innocent people on whom to blame our personal failures and problems. We are now going to consider another answer: society cannot accommodate people whose views about the proper *means* to universal ends are radically different. Many practical disagreements can be resolved through dialogue and compromise. But many cannot. The Catholic and the communist both claim to be concerned with promoting social justice. But their views on the precise nature of social justice and on how to bring it about are so different, so opposed, that they cannot coexist comfortably with each other in the same society. Each is committed to minimizing or even destroying the influence of the other; each feels that to tolerate the other would be morally weak. Now, not all practical disagreements are as profound as those between these two seekers of social justice. Still, many otherwise decent men have come to the conclusion that ideological pluralism, religious or otherwise, is unhealthy or even impossible. These men are not bigoted or prejudiced; they want very much to be tolerant. Many of them are intellectuals, scholars; many of them have fought for worthy causes. But they are convinced that, for practical reasons, all forms of heterodoxy must be crushed, even those we liberals have accepted as innocuous. The ability to accept religious pluralism is a necessary condition of religious tolerance. Unfortunately, the enemy of religious pluralism, as we shall now see, regards it as being as dangerous as religious relativism.

AN ARGUMENT AGAINST RELIGIOUS PLURALISM

Near the end of his study *The Belief of Catholics*, the well-known Catholic intellectual Ronald Knox considers an objection that liberals often raise against the Catholic church: 'Is it just, since thought is free, to penalise *in any way* differences of speculative outlook? Ought not every Church, however powerful, to act as a body corporate within the State, exercising no form of coercion except that of exclusion from its own spiritual privileges? It is very plain that this has not been the Catholic theory in times past. There has been, in Catholic nations, a definite alliance between the secular and the spiritual power.' Knox, writing here in 1927, refuses to be conciliatory, to appease the liberals:

You cannot bind over the Catholic Church, as the price of your adhesion to her doctrines, to waive all right of invoking the secular arm in defence of her own principles ... You have to assume, for practical purposes, a country with a very strong Catholic majority, the overwhelming body of the nation. Probably (though not certainly) you would have to assume that the non-Catholic minority are innovators, newly in revolt against the Catholic system ... Given such circumstances, is it certain that the Catholic Government of the nation would have no right to insist on Catholic education being universal (which is a form of coercion), and even to report or imprison those who unsettled the minds of its subjects with new doctrines?

It is certain that the Church would claim that right for the Catholic Government, even if considerations of prudence forbade its exercise in fact. The Catholic Church will not be one amongst the philosophies. Her children believe, not that her doctrines may be true, but that they *are* true, and consequently part of the normal make-up of a man's mind; not even a parent can legitimately refuse such education to his child. They recognize, however, that such truths (unlike the mathematical axioms) can be argued against; that simple minds can easily be seduced by the sophistries of plausible error; they recognise, further, that the divorce between speculative belief and practical conduct is a divorce in thought, not in fact; that the unchecked development of false theories results in ethical aberrations – Anabaptism yesterday, Bolshevism today – which are a menace even to the social order. And for those reasons a body of Catholic patriots, entrusted with the Government of a Catholic State, will not shrink even from repressive measures in order to perpetuate the secure domination of Catholic principles among their fellow-countrymen.

It is frequently argued, that if Catholics have at the back of their system such notions of 'toleration,' it is unreasonable in them to complain when a modern State restricts, in its turn, the political or educational liberty which they themselves wish to enjoy. What is sauce for the goose is sauce, surely, for the gander. The contention is ill-conceived. For, when we demand liberty in the modern State, we are appealing to its own principles, not to ours. The theory of the modern State is that all religions should be equally tolerated, as long as they do not disturb the peace or otherwise infringe the secular laws of the country; we only claim to share that right amongst the rest.[1]

Such statements have done much to drive liberal intellectuals out of the Catholic church and to lead liberal Protestants, Jews, and atheists to ridicule the church and warn us about the impending return of the spirit of the Inquisition. Nevertheless, we have to admire the late Monsignor Knox for his bluntness, for calling a spade a spade, even if he was writing at a time when the church was less concerned about its public image than it is today. What Knox is saying is that the Catholic church cannot and will not ever accept the modern democratic theory of religious toleration and religious liberty. When it has the power, it will force Catholicism on anyone and everyone that it can. But in a country like Canada or the United States, where Protestants, Jews, and atheists are very influential, it will keep a low profile, use persuasion rather than force in trying to suppress heterodoxy and win converts, and quietly demand that the same toleration that is extended to the tolerant churches also, in the name of consistency, be extended to the Catholic church.

Knox is not concerned with the fact that many non-Catholics generally have high ethical ideals. Nor is he concerned with the fact that the church's traditional policy, which Knox here defends, has resulted in much persecution, suffering, and death. He tells us that the church 'will not be one amongst the philosophies,' that in his view her doctrines are 'part of the normal make-up of a man's mind.' In his view the church must check the development of 'false' (that is, non-

Catholic) theories, for such theories eventually lead to 'ethical aberrations.' Now, Knox's theory has all sorts of interesting philosophical and political implications, but we are going to concentate our attention on his view that religious pluralism is unhealthy, dangerous. At the heart of his argument is his assertion that 'the divorce between speculative belief and practical conduct is a divorce in thought, not in fact; that the unchecked development of false theories results in ethical aberrations ...'

Knox is right in arguing that speculative belief influences practical conduct. The Marxist, Catholic, Jew, and atheistic liberal are all concerned with love, wisdom, justice, peace, and so forth, but their different metaphysical outlooks have led them to different conceptions of the proper means to these ideal ethical ends. The unchecked development of at least certain speculative theories must inevitably result in what a Roman Catholic like Knox must perceive as ethical aberrations. A Catholic and an atheist can agree on many important things; for example, they can both believe that the interests of human beings are more important than the interests of flies. But consider the cases of abortion and divorce. A Catholic believes that the unborn are persons, human beings, and that they have souls; an atheist who considers abortion on demand morally acceptable has a different theory of personality and a different view about souls. For the Catholic, there are theological obstacles to looking favourably on liberal divorce laws; those who approve of liberal divorce laws do so partly because they see no theological obstacles.

Why, then, does the liberal reject Knox's theory? Here are some reasons that immediately come to mind. 1 / The liberal takes freedom of thought, freedom of conscience, much more seriously than Knox does. Knox approves of certain extreme forms of coercion; he has argued that this coercion is necessary for the protection of ideals that take precedence over freedom of thought. He and the liberal disagree about which ideals are the most important. So while the liberal sees Knox as intolerant, Knox sees the liberal as indiscriminately tolerant. 2 / The liberal does not agree with Knox's view that Catholic doctrines are part of the normal make-up of a man's mind. The majority of liberals are not Roman Catholics. Even Catholic liberals reject Knox's view, for though they believe that the church's doctrines are true, they do not regard the non-Catholic as 'abnormal.' 3 / The liberal does not believe that the non-Catholic's arguments are 'sophistries' in a way that the Catholic propagandist's are not. 4 / The liberal does not share Knox's view of what counts as an ethical aberration. Most liberals consider the Inquisition as important an ethical aberration as Anabaptism or even Bolshevism. 5/The liberal is apt to reject Knox's view that a liberal society is morally obliged to tolerate (what Knox has unwisely portrayed as) an intolerant institution; he is likely to feel that Knox has confused genuine tolerance with indiscriminate tolerance.

Knox may not see himself as intolerant. But we can see that arguments like his have encouraged the persecution of religious minorities. In a society that respects freedom of thought, freedom of conscience, a man like Knox is not very dangerous, but in a society that is, say, overwhelmingly Catholic or Moslem or materialistic, people who talk in the way Knox does can successfully promote totalitarianism, religious hatred, and oppression of minorities. Yet, interestingly enough, even some liberals have toyed with the idea that true religious commitment cannot survive in a pluralistic society. One finds, for example, an interesting similarity between Knox's line of reasoning and that of a man revered by liberals, the American journalist Walter Lippmann.

RELIGIOUS PLURALISM AND SECULARISM

A section of Lippmann's 1929 study *A Preface to Morals* is devoted to an analysis of 'The Logic of Toleration.' As we consider the following passages from this section, we should bear in mind that though they were written at roughly the same time as the statements of Knox that we have just considered, they represent the views of a liberal journalist rather than a conservative Catholic apologist.

As a result of the great religious wars the governing classes were forced to realize that unless they consented to the policy of toleration they would be ruined. There is no reason to suppose that except among a few idealists toleration has ever been much admired as a principle. It was originally, and in large measure it still is, nothing but a practical necessity. For in its interior life no church can wholly admit that its rivals may provide an equally good vehicle of salvation ...

As a consequence of the modern theory of religious freedom the churches find themselves in an anomalous position. Inwardly, to their communicants, they continue to assert that they possess the only complete version of the truth. But outwardly, in their civic relations with other churches and with the civil power, they preach and practice toleration. The separation of church and state involves more than a mere logical difficulty for the churchman. It involves a deep psychological difficulty for the members of the congregation. As communicants they are expected to believe without reservation that their church is the only true means of salvation; otherwise the multitude of separate sects would be meaningless. But as citizens they are expected to maintain a neutral indifference to the claims of all the sects, and to resist encroachments by any one sect upon the religious practices of the others. This is the best compromise which human wisdom has as yet devised, but it has one inevitable consequence which the superficial advocates of toleration often overlook. It is difficult to remain warmly convinced that the authority of any one sect is divine, when as a matter of daily experience all sects have to be treated alike ...

The human soul is not so divided in compartments that a man can be indifferent in one part of his soul and firmly believing in another. The existence of rival sects, the visible demonstration that none has a monopoly, the habit of neutrality, cannot but dispose men against an unquestioning acceptance of the authority of one sect. So many faiths, so many loyalties, are offered to the modern man that at last none seems to him wholly inevitable and fixed in the order of the universe. The existence of many churches in one community weakens the foundation of all of them. And that is why every church in the heyday of its power proclaims itself to be catholic and intolerant ...

But when there are many churches in the same community, none can make wholly good the claim that it is catholic. None has the power to discipline the individual which a universal church exercises. For, as Dr. Figgis puts it, when many churches are tolerated: 'excommunication has ceased to be tyrannical by becoming futile.'[2]

In the next section of the book, Lippmann talks about 'A Working Compromise,' the public school:

Under [the prevailing theory of the public school] the schools are silent about matters of faith, and teachers are supposed to be neutral on the issues of history and science which bear upon religion. The churches permit this because they cannot agree on the dogma they would wish to have taught. The Catholics would rather have no dogma in the schools than Protestant dogma; the fundamentalists would rather have none than have modernist. But that is only because all the alternatives are so much worse. No church can sincerely subscribe to the theory that questions of faith do not enter into the education of children ...

As a matter of fact non-sectarianism is a useful political phrase rather than an accurate description of what goes on in the schools. If there is teaching of science, that teaching is by implication almost always agnostic. The fundamentalists point this out, and they are quite right. The teaching of history, under a so-called non-sectarian policy, is usually [in the United States] a rather diluted Protestant version of history. The Catholics are quite right when they point this out ...

But the chief effect of the non-sectarian policy is to weaken sectarian attachment, to wean the child from the faith of his fathers by making him feel that patriotism somehow demands that he shall not press his convictions too far, that commonsense and good-fellowship mean that he must not be too absolute. The leaders of the churches are aware of this peril. Every once in a while they make an effort to combat it.[3]

Finally, Lippmann speaks about 'The Dissolution of a Sovereignty':

In place of one church which is sovereign over all men, there are now many rival churches, rival states, voluntary associations, and detached individuals ...

Religion has become for most modern men one phase in a varied experience; it no longer regulates their civic duties, their economic activities, their family life, and their opinions. It has ceased to have universal dominion, and is now held to be supreme only within its own domain. But there is much uncertainty as to what that domain is. In actual affairs, the religious obligations of modern men are often weaker than their social interests and generally weaker than the fiercer claims of patriotism ...

However reverent they may be when they are in their churches, [men] no longer feel wholly assured when they listen to the teaching that these are the words of the ministers of a heavenly king.[4]

In these interesting passages, Lippmann has raised a variety of political, theological, and philosophical problems, and some of them we shall be considering in detail in later chapters. Here, though, we want to focus our attention on Lippmann's main thesis, that toleration, in the form of acceptance of religious pluralism, inevitably leads to 'secularism' and the decline of *all* religions.

Unlike Knox, Lippmann is making no value-judgments. He is trying to give an accurate *description* of some important phenomena. He believes that the things that he is saying here can and must be accepted as true by both friends of religion and enemies of religion. Yet, while he himself has not made any value-judgments, he has provided people like Ronald Knox with a theoretical justification of their hostility towards the liberal theory of toleration. If Lippmann has made sound observations, then it is highly imprudent of powerful churches to encourage or even accept the kind of religious pluralism that people in our society have become accustomed to. But are Lippmann's observations sound?

Lippmann starts out on the wrong foot by arguing that history teaches us that political toleration of religious minorities has generally been nothing but a practical necessity. Though a liberal, Lippmann seems to have a theory of human nature here which is closer to Hobbes's than to Locke's. In his view, men practise tolerance unwillingly; they would not tolerate minorities if they did not have to. But Lippmann has ignored a great deal of relevant data. The policy of toleration predates the wars of the post-Reformation period. Many ancient and medieval theocracies were intolerant *in spite of* the 'practical necessity' to be tolerant. The medieval wars between the Christians and the Moslems, for example, proved to be damaging to both. Some ancient and medieval societies, however, were tolerant even though they could have afforded to be intolerant. For example, the Persian Empire under Cyrus was rather liberal in its treatment of religious minorities. All of the principal religions of the world have preached toleration in some form. Even the medieval Christians and the earliest Moslems showed themselves capable of putting up with religious minorities at various times.

Lippmann has probably underestimated the number of idealists in the world too. Consider the modern example of the French. France has always been a predominantly Roman Catholic country; yet, one of the effects of the Dreyfus Affair was a strong reaction against the influence of the Church of Rome in French life. The French have not *had* to be any more tolerant than the Spanish, but their record in the area of religious toleration has been significantly better. Moreover, it is not clear why Lippmann believes that tolerating religious minorities requires a powerful church to admit that its rivals may provide an equally good vehicle of salvation. Though, as I shall point out later, the doctrine of 'exclusive salvation' is indirectly an obstacle to religious tolerance, being tolerant does not require one to abandon that doctrine. In a pluralistic society, men can still worry about their personal destiny; and they can still enjoy believing that they will be 'saved' while unbelievers will not.

Again, it is not clear why acceptance of religious pluralism should produce a deep psychological difficulty for churchmen. (For a man who professes to be ethical, or, in some cases, sincerely religious, persecuting men of other faiths should produce deeper psychological difficulties.) Lippmann keeps assuming that the man who is willing to accept religious pluralism must be a religious relativist. But why does the Christian's willingness to tolerate (rather than *respect*) unbelievers require him to believe that Christian leaders do not possess the only complete version of the truth? Why does it require him to be 'indifferent'? The habit of religious toleration need not dispose a man against an unquestioning acceptance of the authority of one sect. In a pluralistic society, men *freely* accept the authority of their chosen leaders. And is that not the way in which they *ought* to accept that authority?

As for Lippmann's statement that the existence of many churches in one community weakens the foundation of all of them, it would appear to be gratuitous, and for a variety of reasons. 1 / Relative separation of church and state certainly has tended to weaken the *political* power of certain churches. But perhaps it has strengthened the *moral* foundation of churches. The moral strength of the Roman Catholic church may well be greater now than it was in the age of the Protestant Reformers. And the fact that the church is no longer burdened with such institutions as the Inquisition has made it a stronger *religious* institution, not a weaker one. It is wrong for modern Catholics to think of the High Middle Ages as the 'good old days.' Anyone who takes the teachings of Jesus seriously can see that the 'good old days' were not so good. 2 / Similarly, it is certainly not obvious that American Catholics or Lutherans today are less sincere in their religious professions than their Spanish Catholic or Swedish Lutheran co-religionists. Indeed something that is freely accepted is apt to be respected more than something that one has been coerced to accept. Lippmann has not convinced me that the 'faith' of the ignorant medieval serf is more profound than that of the modern reflective believer. 3 / Why does Lippmann believe that churches in a pluralistic society can no longer make 'wholly good' the claim that they alone are catholic? Jews or Lutherans or Catholics still believe that their religion is the true or best religion. They believe that their church *ought to be* catholic. Even in the Middle Ages, no church actually was catholic in the sense of being universally accepted as the one true church. Since the time of Mohammed, Christians and Moslems have been well aware that there are rival churches. And even before Mohammed, Christianity was not the universally accepted religion. 4 / For reasons I shall explain in a later chapter, I cannot accept Lippmann's naïve view that the 'meaningfulness' of the 'multitude of separate sects' depends on their promise of some kind of exclusive salvation. He simply does not understand the complexity of religious commitment.

Lippmann believes that religious pluralism breeds secularism by weakening the religious commitment of all men in the political community. It is not obvious to me that religious commitment in the modern world has been steadily 'declining.' I suppose that Lippmann and I have different ideas about what constitutes a *genuine* religious commitment. But I can say, without a moment's hesitation, that the last two hundred years have produced some of the most religious men in the history of the world: Kierkegaard, Cardinal Newman, Schweitzer, Bonhoeffer, Buber. And I also want to question Lippmann's theory about the origins of secularism. In my view, secularism has more often *given rise* to religious pluralism than resulted from it. Ask yourself why religious sects come into existence in the first place. When the Protestant Reformers attacked the Roman church, it was largely because they were genuinely convinced that the church had become too worldly, too secular. The Protestant Reformers sought to revive the spirit of the earliest Christians. In their eyes, the Church of Rome was corrupt and was no longer faithful to the teachings of Jesus. Similarly, Christianity arose at a time when certain Jews were convinced that the Pharisaic leaders were making a mockery of the teachings of the Law and the Prophets. And so the plurality of religious denominations is a testament to a long series of attempts to protect the sacred from the encroachments of the profane, to protect the spiritual from the infringements of the secular. Lippmann may be right in believing that there is a causal relationship between secularism and religious pluralism; but the causal arrow does not go in the direction that he thinks it does.

Lippmann has also misunderstood the role of the public school in a democratic, pluralistic society. He can only see the public school as an instrument of secularization. But what is its real function? Public schools originated out of a need to provide education for people who could not afford to pay for a sound education in a private school (religious or otherwise). In the Middle Ages, or even in the last century, leaders did not appreciate the importance of giving every child the kind of education that would enable him to lead a rich, rewarding life. In our society, we are more enlightened in this respect; we see that every child has a right to learn how to read and write, appreciate art and music, relate with children from different backgrounds, and so forth. We recognize that education is the key to civilization. If churches had provided adequate education for all children, public schools would never have become popular. And in our society, there is ample opportunity for religious denominations to provide religious education for their young. People are permitted to send their children to religious schools instead of or in addition to public schools. If religious schools cannot compete with public schools, it is largely because religious people have failed in their responsibility to support the religious schools of their church. It is also partly because religious education is usually less impressive than it should be. (I know many graduates of Catholic and Jewish schools who are committed atheists and bitter critics of all religion.)

Lippmann is right when he says that non-sectarianism is a useful political phrase rather than an accurate description of what actually goes on in the public schools. Public school teaching can never be absolutely neutral on religious questions; most religious doctrines are so broad that they spill over into the various departments of knowledge – science, history, literature, and so on. Still, parents and clergymen have ample opportunity to influence the child by setting forth their side of the story. The worst public schools have had the healthy effect of forcing parents and clergymen to think more critically and find better methods of getting their own message across to children. Moreover, in countries like the United States and Canada, the public schools tend to be supportive of religion per se, to encourage young people to believe that religious commitment is basically a healthy and positive thing. In this sense, atheists have much more to complain about in the public schools than religious people have.

It is certainly not obvious that the non-sectarian policy of the public schools inevitably results in the weakening of religious commitment. If religious values are superior to those to which a child is exposed in a public school, then a reasonably intelligent child should be able to see so when he contrasts the 'secularism' of his public school with the religious life of his home or church. It is not clear that graduates of public schools generally end up as rabid patriots. (Some of the most offensive nationalists that I have encountered have been products of parochial schools.) The authoritarian methods of religious schools often produce the opposite effect that they were supposed to produce. (I know many Catholics who would have grown up to respect Catholicism if they had not been sent to study with incompetent Catholic teachers in a second-rate separate school.) Certainly the public schools teach that one should not press one's convictions *too far*; if religious schools had done the same over the centuries, there would have been considerably less religious persecution than the human community was exposed to. But in any case, the moral education in the public schools reflects the Jewish-Greek-Christian values that pervade (at least as ideals) the society at large.

'Religion,' Lippmann tells us, 'has become for most modern men one phase in a varied experience; it no longer regulates their civic duties, their economic activities, their family life, and their opinions. It has ceased to have universal dominion, and is now held to be supreme only within its own domain.' These remarks are misleading. For one thing, they undervalue traditional distinctions between the sacred and the profane, the spiritual and the worldly. 'Then give to Caesar what is Caesar's, but give to God what is God's' (Matthew 22:21). Christian theologians have had bitter disputes over the real meaning of these words; still, these words do point in a certain direction. Christianity developed and flourished in a non-theocratic (or at least non-Christian) society. The economic and political schemes of the medieval Christian church eventually did it more harm than good. There was, after all, nothing intrinsically *Christian* in medieval feudalism. For the contemporary Christian who lives in a pluralistic society, however, religion *does* play a role in regulating his civic duties, economic activities, family life, and opinions. A truly committed Christian will not ignore his civic responsibilities, cheat his customers, abuse his children, or believe that exploitation and persecution are morally acceptable. In a pluralistic society like ours, the leaders of a particular church cannot force members of the church to do things in the way that leaders of a theocracy can. But they can teach and advise and guide. And through their teaching, they continue to exert a profound influence on the opinions of those who look to them for guidance. So for the contemporary Christian or Moslem or Jew or Buddhist, religion has – perhaps more than ever before – something close to 'universal dominion.' All we have to do is pick up the daily newspaper to see how many religious men are still willing to suffer or die rather than tolerate the injustices perpetrated by corrupt tyrants. (Most religious men are not as morally aggressive as they should be, but that is an old story.)

RELIGIOUS PLURALISM VS RELIGIOUS RELATIVISM

'In place of one church which is sovereign over all men, there are now many rival churches, rival states, voluntary associations, and detached individuals.' Here Lippmann has given us an accurate description of our own pluralistic society. Lippmann sees our policy of pluralism and toleration as 'the best compromise which human wisdom has as yet devised'; but he has mixed feelings, even in spite of his basic liberalism. Knox, in contrast, finds the present state of affairs rather depressing. Knox believes that the world would be a better place if the Church of

Rome were sovereign over all men. I suppose he should; after all, he is a Roman Catholic priest. Unlike Knox, Lippmann and I cannot ignore the negative aspects of the medieval culture that was dominated by the Roman church.

When we seek to defend our social system, we sooner or later point out that ours is a 'free society.' There is, of course, no absolute freedom in any society. But ours is relatively free. We have a substantial amount of freedom of thought, religious freedom, and freedom of choice. Freedom may not be the most important thing in our life, but it is important enough, and we are understandably reluctant to forfeit the fundamental freedoms that our ancestors have fought so hard for. Freedom of choice means being able to pick from among a reasonably broad range of alternatives. Hobson's choice is no choice at all. Choosing to accept a particular religious way of life or die is not much of a choice either.

Some honest competition among religions may well be a healthy thing, for consider these points: 1 / Leaders in a theocracy do not have to worry about learning from 'the competition.' In a theocracy, the competition has, for all intents and purposes, been wiped out; the Established Church is essentially the only game in town. You can take it or leave it, and if you leave it, you are in deep trouble. With enlightened leadership, a theocracy can be a progressive, civilized political community; but enlightened leaders are, alas, few and far between, and men of limited vision have a way of gaining control of the state. 2 / We take pride in having made a religious *commitment*. It is difficult to take pride in one's beliefs or actions when one knows that they have been forced upon oneself. 3 / In a pluralistic society, religious denominations *are* involved in a kind of competition. Leaders of every particular church believe that theirs is the true or best church, and they want other men to come to agree with them on this point. No religious denomination is thoroughly exclusivistic, as we shall see in a later chapter; every church seeks proselytes, converts, though churches have radically different methods of proselytizing. When the method of making converts involves force, deception, or threats, the church that is using it is guilty of ruthless competition. There are, however, healthy ways to go about attracting people to one's religious denomination. The healthiest of all is to set a good example that people will want to follow.

Though it ends with the suffix '-ism,' religious *pluralism* is not just a theory or ideology; it is a fact, a state of affairs. 'The Catholic Church,' Monsignor Knox informs us, 'will not be one amongst the philosophies.'

Well, it may not want to be, but, as a matter of fact, it *is* and always *will be*. And the same holds true of every other church. For history teaches us that no matter how much power a tyrannical regime has, it cannot completely destroy heterodoxy.

Enemies of religious pluralism always make one of two mistakes. Either they assume that religious pluralism will inevitably lead to religious relativism or, worse yet, they see acceptance of the fact of religious pluralism as a manifestation of religious relativism. Those who associate religious tolerance with religious relativism play right into the hands of people like Knox.

The man who rejects religious relativism is the man who believes that his faith is, if not the one true faith, the best that he can have. But the man who rejects religious pluralism is the man who believes that men of different faiths cannot live together harmoniously. The enemy of pluralism is an enemy of freedom of thought and freedom of choice; the enemy of relativism is simply an enemy of indifference. Yet, the following valid objection can be raised: the non-relativist does reject pluralism in at least one sense, for he believes that men of other faiths *ought* to accept his. Now, there are actually some people who are happy about the fact that other men do not share their faith. But most religious people seem to believe that the world would be a better place if men of other faiths came over to their side. Fair enough: the tolerant man is not usually very happy about the fact of religious pluralism. But he *accepts* it. There are limits to what he will do to make converts.

5

Proselytizing and intolerance

The connection between religious persecution and religious propaganda is not intuitively obvious. We tend to associate religious persecution with its most obvious forms, murder and torture, exploitation and segregation. If we find religious propaganda distasteful, we nevertheless accept it as an aspect of the 'free exchange of ideas.' But many forms of missionary activity and overassertive 'witnessing' accompany, foreshadow, and promote more radical forms of religious harassment. There is something essentially intolerant about the missionary, the proselytizer. He has much more trouble than the average religious believer in accepting the fact that men of other faiths and philosophical persuasions do not share his religious convictions. And unlike the philosophical apologist, he is impatient and feels that it is urgent that religious outsiders immediately embrace his religious outlook. His impatience often leads him to eschew the safe but slow method of rational persuasion in favour of unwholesome methods of winning converts, methods that border on and lead up to persecution. A man with a 'mission' often degenerates into a dangerous fanatic. C.E.M. Joad has articulated the relevant psychological insight: 'All persecution, it is not too much to say all propaganda, arises from the curious inability of the human mind to think anything by itself. Directly we hold a belief to be true we desire to communicate it to others, directly we think such and such things desirable we endeavour to make others think them desirable also.' What Joad says of the philosopher is equally applicable to the unreflective missionary or propagandist: 'No philosopher is really content with the conviction that he has found truth. He is lonely with truth and is not content until others share it. Hence propaganda, and, in extreme cases, persecution.'[1]

We usually do not like the people who come to convert us. We often find them arrogant, ignorant, hypocritical, meddlesome. One does not have to be a religious relativist to resent the fact that missionaries and proselytizers have made little effort to understand the depth of our own personal religious commitments. We are prepared to listen to them, but we soon lose our patience when we find that they are not prepared to listen to us. Dialogue, yes; monologue, no. Education, fair; deception and sophistry, foul. Most of us are also well aware of the fact that proselytizers have not always been as pleasant and respectful as most of those who visit us at home now in our democratic, pluralistic society. In the past, they have been prepared to take extreme measures to enlighten us, to save our souls; outsiders, 'heretics,' 'infidels,' 'unbelievers' have been tortured, burnt at the stake, and deprived of civil liberties. Yet, even many respectable religious leaders have failed to appreciate the connection between proselytizing and intolerance. Under what conditions is religious proselytizing morally acceptable? When is it morally advisable? And when is it morally unacceptable?

UTILITARIAN CONSIDERATIONS

In any given case of proselytizing or attempted proselytizing, there is a person (P) who is committed to a doctrine or set of doctrines (x) and is actively seeking to convert another person or group of people (Q) from not believing x to believing x. Q may or may not be committed to a doctrine or set of doctrines that directly conflicts with x; conversion does not necessarily involve abandoning some of one's older beliefs (other than not-x), although it may. From a utilitarian standpoint, Q's conversion is morally good if and only if it promotes the general happiness, while it is morally right for P to (attempt to) proselytize Q if and only if P's actions here are based on his *reasonable* belief that Q's believing x will be conducive to an increase in the total general happiness. 'Act-utilitarians' believe that we should consider each particular case on its own merits, and 'rule-utilitarians' are concerned primarily with the morality of either the general institution of proselytizing or the general effort to convert people to believing x.[2] So for the act-utilitarian, the key moral question here is whether or not P's actions do actually promote the general happiness, and for the rule-utilitarian, the key moral question is whether or not (attempted) proselytizing is, as a general rule, conducive to an increase in the general happiness. What we must consider now is how P's (attempted) proselytizing of Q can be conducive to an increase or decrease in the general happiness.

A utilitarian could defend proselytizing on a wide variety of grounds:

psychological, social, and metaphysical. The psychotherapeutic value of religious belief is acknowledged even by certain militant atheists. For many people, their religious beliefs are a source of contentment, of peace of mind. Religion helps them to bear the misfortunes of life, to feel more at ease with nature and their fellow human beings. It gives them a sense of purpose. In short, it often helps to make people 'healthy-minded.' And just as abandoning atheism may lead to peace of mind, abandoning one set of religious beliefs in favour of another may also have positive psychotherapeutic results. Proselytizers do not often use this argument when they are attempting to convert people, although P might say to Q in passing, 'If you believe x, you will, I promise you, find life more pleasant, more satisfying.' Missionaries tend to be more concerned with truth and salvation than with the mental health of potential proselytes, but if you asked them to defend their actions, they might argue that even if x is not true, Q is still better off for believing x.

Conversion can have social value too. Throughout history, many men have converted in order to be 'successful' in the political, business, or professional world. In certain places, 'advancement' depends partly on the church in which one worships. Of course, conversions of this kind are not always sincere. The proselytizer wants Q to believe x, not simply to pretend that he believes x. Still, a utilitarian theorist might well argue that if Q's not believing x prevents a talented man like Q from fulfilling his natural potential as a leader in some field, then P's proselytizing Q is probably conducive to an increase in the general happiness. Again, P is probably more concerned with truth and salvation than with Q's personal advancement and social utility, but if you pressed him to defend his proselytizing, he might tell you that even if x is not true, he is still performing a service for both Q and society by proselytizing.

It is important to see that increasing the general happiness does not necessarily require increasing Q's happiness. P can persuasively argue that even if his (attempted) proselytizing makes Q substantially unhappier, it may still be conducive to the *general* happiness. For in addition to considering Q's happiness, P, if a utilitarian, is obliged to consider his own happiness and the happiness of all those who would like (or not like) to see Q believe x. Critics of proselytizing missionaries usually fail to appreciate the psychotherapeutic value that the proselytizer's activity has for the proselytizer himself. If the Jehovah's Witnesses or Mormons do not make me substantially unhappier by vainly trying to convert me, and since it obviously makes them happy to be doing the kind of proselytizing that they are doing, their proselytizing would seem, all other things being equal, to be conducive to an increase in the general happiness. When I let the Jehovah's Witnesses give me their little speech, I may well be helping them to enjoy peace of mind, to feel important, and at a low price. But are all other things equal? The actual conversion of a person affects a wide range of people, not just the proselytizer and the proselyte. It may be a source of unhappiness to Q's family, friends, former co-religionists, and others. Proselytizers, even when they are utilitarians, rarely take such matters into consideration. And in any event, many people find attempts to convert them singularly unpleasant.

A utilitarian could attack proselytizing on the very same grounds on which other utilitarians defend it. In abandoning his earlier religious (or atheistic) beliefs in favour of x, Q may have done psychological and social harm both to himself and to others. As a result of his conversion, Q may now be *less* capable of bearing the misfortunes of life. He may have alienated relatives, old friends, and former co-religionists. He may have burdened himself with feelings of guilt that are an obstacle to peace of mind. Though he no longer will be regarded as a heretic by P and P's co-religionists, he will now appear to loved ones as an apostate, an infidel. Moreover, 'outsiders' often tend to be suspicious of proselytes; Q may now be regarded by many as a disloyal, weak, and opportunistic individual. Some outsiders will see Q's conversion as a personal matter, but others will perceive it as a reflection of some weakness in Q's character, or even of emotional instability. Some resent converts for the same reasons that they resent missionaries. Educated people also often believe that there is a core of moral truths in all major religions, and they may well interpret Q's conversion as an act rooted in his ignorance and misunderstanding of his former faith.

The missionary's ultimate utilitarian argument is that if Q believes x, Q will be 'saved.' 'Salvation' is a rather nebulous concept. Few proselytizers are prepared to spell out in detail exactly what happens to a person when he is saved. Salvation is sometimes associated with things that we have or seek in this world, for instance, relief from guilt, peace of mind, times of bliss, awareness of being loved, the ability to love. It is often associated with immortality, eternal life. And sometimes it is associated with coming closer to God, so that to be saved is to find God or have a vision of God or be near to God. Still, no matter what specific benefits salvation brings, it would certainly seem to be in our interest to be saved. People are willing to be persecuted and killed if they sincerely believe that their faith will be rewarded with immortality, nearness to God, and so on. Compared to such rewards, pleasure and 'success' are relatively unimportant. But how can a potential proselyte like Q be sure that P is telling him the truth when P says that believing x is the exclusive way to achieve salvation? And how can Q be sure that the religious beliefs he would have to abandon are *not* necessary for achieving salvation? For that matter, how can he be sure that salvation will actually compensate him for all the things that he will have to give up when he lives according to x? There is empirical evidence to justify the proselytizer's claim that believing x *may* lead to peace of mind and 'success.' But as even an amateur philosophical theologian knows, no one has yet come up with a convincing proof that an afterlife awaits those who hold certain metaphysical and ethical beliefs. If Q accepts the Bible (or some other work) as revelation, P can try to show Q that certain passages therein suggest that believing x is the key to salvation. But there are missionaries of many faiths making use of different interpretations of passages of many different 'sacred' works.

Having considered psychological, social, and metaphysical grounds, we can see that from a rule-utilitarian standpoint, it would seem to be extremely difficult or even impossible to determine whether or not proselytizing as an institution is basically morally sound. Even determining whether converting people to some *specific* doctrine is morally sound looks like a difficult task. The act-utilitarian's job, of course, is in one way much easier than the rule-utilitarian's, for he can deal with each case of (attempted) proselytizing on its own merits. But not only does the act-utilitarian have a huge number of individual cases to consider, but determining the moral rightness of a particular act of proselytizing may require a fantastic number of calculations involving a very large number of factors or variables.

But to turn to non-utilitarian considerations now would be premature; for in addition to considering psychological, social, and metaphysical grounds, the utilitarian must consider yet another aspect of proselytizing, which involves the specific content of the doctrine or set of doctrines in question. In many cases Q's coming to believe x will clearly make him a morally better human being. So far we have ignored the specific content of x and have thought of P and Q as two highly civilized men. But proselytizing does not always involve ignorant young Jehovah's Witnesses trying to convert highly civilized people. Consider, for example, the case of the missionary, P_1, who knows that certain savages, Q_1, in some exotic locality not only do not love their neighbours but torture people outside the tribe, sacrifice such outsiders to their god, and occasionally eat them. Some of these bizarre rituals may reflect Q_I's religious beliefs; Q_I may believe that if a young virgin is not sacrificed at least once a week, Q_I's god will become angry and destroy Q_I. Now let us assume that no matter how happy Q_I is as a result of sacrificing the young virgins, Q_I's happiness does not compensate for the unhappiness of the young virgins or others. Would it not seem morally advisable for P_I to convince Q_I that there is only one, benevolent God, who does not require or even like human sacrifice? Tolerance, as we have seen, does not demand that we condone human sacrifice, torture, cannibalism, and similar practices; if anything, tolerance demands that we *not* condone such practices. So from a utilitarian standpoint, it may well be morally advisable for P to attempt to proselytize Q, and whether it is or not depends upon how highly civilized Q is and what the specific content of x is. We would not have much use for a missionary who converted savages to Christianity by convincing them that Christianity does not conflict with the inhuman rituals that they practise; such a 'conversion' would not be worth very much, even if the savages had bothered to memorize every word of the Bible.

From a utilitarian standpoint, however, it may well be morally advisable under certain conditions for P *not* to attempt to proselytize Q, for it is not difficult to think of a case in which Q's coming to believe x will make him a morally *worse* human being. If an enlightened person from the west (Q) leaves a tribe of savages having himself been convinced that human sacrifice is a wholesome practice, the witch doctor (P) who converted him has not done much to promote the general happiness. A *pure* ethical relativist cannot see the point of any proselytizing; but anyone who believes that there are certain ethical absolutes is surely committed, in principle, to appreciating the value of *some* proselytizing.

'Ethical' proselytizing cannot, of course, be completely isolated from religious or metaphysical proselytizing, in so far as ethical, religious, and metaphysical *beliefs* interact and mutually influence one another. Believing in the existence of a just and loving God may be the cause *or* effect of certain moral attitudes. Moreover, in many cultures, failure to observe certain purely symbolic rituals is widely regarded as being just as immoral as theft or even murder. Most religious people regard religious duties (that is, duties to God or some god) as ethical duties in the same way as they regard duties to their fellow man. An important theme in the Gospels is the conflict between Jesus and certain Pharisees over which commandments of the Pentateuch are most important. The Pharisees described in the Gospels refuse to subordinate rules concerning, say, the Sabbath to broad ethical rules relating to concern for the interests of one's fellow human beings. Throughout the centuries, much religious persecution and propaganda have had their roots in minor doctrinal or theological disagreements rather than broad ethical disagreements. For example, those who sought to convert or destroy the Anabaptists during the sixteenth century believed that the Anabaptists were dangerous, immoral people – relatively 'uncivilized' – because of their heterodox views on baptism, religious liberty, and so forth.

Now, I am no religious relativist, and I realize that to dismiss such disagreements as 'minor' may seem to be begging the question. But consider this point: to their persecutors the Anabaptists were different from headhunters in degree rather than in kind; for in the eyes of these persecutors, rebaptism was *immoral*, even if less so than something like headhunting. We who live in the twentieth century can now see that the sixteenth-century Anabaptists were, by and large, if perhaps mistaken in their views, highly civilized people; proselytizing would probably not have made them morally better people. But the fact remains that there is no clear line of demarcation between 'ethical' proselytizing and this other questionable kind of proselytizing. For even if we reject the pure ethical relativist's claim that there are no transcultural ideals, no ethical absolutes, we must still recognize that people in different religious denominations disagree about what is necessary for the realization of these ideals. The Jehovah's Witness certainly believes that if he can convert the Catholic or the Presbyterian, he will make him a morally better person.

Nevertheless, the moral justifiability of an act of proselytizing does not ultimately rest on the missionary's 'opinions' as to what beliefs it is morally advisable to hold. Few people believe that beliefs about morality are articles of faith in the way that beliefs about salvation are. Rational discourse on moral subjects is quite common, indeed an everyday matter. A large part of being civilized, as we agreed earlier, involves being able to give good reasons for believing that one should do this rather than that. If the Jehovah's Witness is going to believe that Q's believing x will make him a morally better person, the Jehovah's Witness ought to be able to discuss in a rational, non-dogmatic way what morality and moral goodness consist in. But many missionaries have difficulty carrying on an extended rational discussion of moral and religious subjects. And that, alas, is why religious teaching has often given way to religious propaganda and why religious propaganda has often given way in turn to religious persecution.

When one considers certain historic attempts to proselytize, such as Christian attempts to convert the Jews and sixteenth-century attempts to convert the Anabaptists, there is good reason to sympathize with the potential proselytes. The Jews and Anabaptists have rarely been as irrational (or immoral) as the fanatics who have come to convert them. In the sixteenth century, for example, if one pressed the leaders of the Jewish and Anabaptist communities, they were able to defend their ethical code with at least as much grace and depth as the missionaries could. Aware of this fact, more 'sophisticated' missionaries turned to sophistry and deception, and the worst of them resorted to threats and violence. So it is not enough for the proselytizer to believe that he can make Q morally better; he must have good reasons for believing that he can, and he must be able to express these reasons when he presents his case to the potential proselyte. If the potential proselyte is wholly irrational, the missionary will not be able to make much *use* of rational arguments in dealing with him. Still, he should be able to provide such arguments. Dealing with Q_1 who is irrational is obviously very different from dealing with Q_2 who is not. But in any case, P should have good reasons for believing that by getting Q to believe x he is making Q a morally better person. If they would listen to me, I could offer savages some excellent reasons why they would be morally better people if they stopped sacrificing young virgins to their god. When proselytizers visit *me*, however, I usually listen closely, but the arguments that they offer are not intellectually exciting.

To recapitulate, we find that when the morality of proselytizing is considered from a utilitarian standpoint, few broad conclusions can be drawn. P's proselytizing of Q may be conducive to an increase in the general happiness for 'psychological,' 'social,' and 'metaphysical' reasons, but for the very same reasons it may also be conducive to a decrease in the total general happiness. Few if any missionaries seem to appreciate the complexity of the utilitarian calculations that are based on a serious consideration of these various factors. The moral rightness (or wrongness) of proselytizing would appear to depend for the utilitarian on the degree to which belief in the *particular* doctrine or set of doctrines in question will 'civilize' the potential proselyte or make him a morally better person. Anyone who is opposed to radical ethical relativism and believes that there is at least one ethical absolute – anyone who takes the idea of civilization seriously – is committed *in principle* to appreciating the value of *some* proselytizing. But since 'ethical' proselytizing cannot be completely isolated from religious or metaphysical proselytizing, and since people of different religious faiths disagree about how to realize ethical ideals, it is extremely difficult for utilitarians to reach a consensus about which proselytizing is morally defensible even on these 'ethical' grounds. Few of us are pure ethical relativists, contemptuous of those missionaries who try to undermine the religious beliefs of savages who have faith in a god who demands human sacrifice, torture, and cannibalism. The Jehovah's Witnesses, regarding all other religious bodies as instruments of Satan, simply believe that the average liberal intellectual is still too relativistic and morally weak. Nevertheless, rational discourse on moral subjects is possible, even common, and a large part of being civilized is being able to give good reasons for believing that one should do (or believe) this as opposed to that. Anyone who is rational enough to be willing to reflect on the morality of missionary activity cannot be expected to have any use for those fanatic, irrational proselytizers whose strongest weapons are sophistry and brute force.

DEONTOLOGICAL CONSIDERATIONS

From a 'deontological' point of view, actions are intrinsically right or wrong, regardless of their consequences; reason dictates that we have certain duties, and one must do his duty even if his doing so will result in unhappiness. The deontologist asks us whether or not the missionary can rightly approve of the proselytizing activities of men who do not share his religious convictions. The most important deontologist, Kant, argues in his ethical writings that the moral wrongness of promise-breaking is reflected in our inability to accept the right to break promises as a universal rule. If everyone broke promises whenever he found it convenient, the very institution of promising would collapse. Now I never cease to be amused at how the very same Roman Catholic friends of mine who look favourably on their church's attempts to convert Jews and Protestants express an implacable hostility to Jehovah's Witnesses, Mormons, and other proselytizers who seek to turn Catholics away from the religion of the Roman church. I am amused, but not surprised; I am amused, I suppose, because I do not share the religious beliefs of my Roman Catholic friends. To most non-Catholics, the attitude of these Catholic friends of mine must seem to be a bit inconsistent, if not hypocritical. Catholics, of course, regard their religious beliefs as true and good; but then, Jehovah's Witnesses and Mormons regard their own religious beliefs as true and good and better than those of Roman Catholics. It is interesting to note that in the Middle Ages the same church that zealously sought converts from Judaism or paganism did not permit non-Christians to attempt to convert Christians and actually condemned non-Christians for proselytizing even when these non-Christians had no strong interest in seeking converts. When two groups of aggressive proselytizers meet, the result is inevitably 'holy war.'

Our concern, though, is not with history at this point, and so let us ask whether it is possible for missionaries to have the attitude that the proselytizing activities of 'outsiders' can be morally wholesome. Proselytizing is obviously not in the same class as promise-breaking, and we can imagine P saying aloud, 'Everyone has a right to attempt to proselytize, and may the best man win.' Still, when P_2 wants to proselytize Q, the very existence of some other 'outside' proselytizer, P_3, is a hindrance to P_2's being successful in his work. For at the same time as P_2 is trying to convert Q, P_3 may be trying to convert Q or even those who share P_2's religious beliefs. Also, Q may argue in the following way: 'Why should I convert, right now, P_2? Perhaps I should first hear what P_3, P_4, and P_5 have to offer in the way of rational arguments. In fact, at this very moment, there are intelligent men attempting to persuade others of the reasonableness of the religious beliefs *I already hold*.' P_2 may well believe that P_3's religious beliefs are as bad as or even worse than those that Q already holds; when this is the case, P_2 must be at least as worried about P_3's proselytizing activities as he is about the fact that Q does not share P_2's religious beliefs. We should not be surprised, then, that proselytizers dislike and fear 'outside' proselytizers, nor should we be surprised at their efforts to undermine the efforts of these other proselytizers.

Now try to imagine a society in which everyone was trying to proselytize everyone else. What kind of society would this be? Every time that P came to convert Q, he would find that Q was also trying to convert *him*. Such a society would be strange indeed. If reason triumphed in such a society, the 'best man' would 'win.' But *could* reason prevail in a society in which *everyone* aimed to *persuade* rather than to *learn*? I suspect that in this imaginary society, proselytizing would give way either to holy war or the abolition of missionary activity. For when people are continually subjected to attempts to convert them, they often react by becoming more liberal and tolerant, and proselytizing comes to appear to them as a silly, futile business. I have often thought that if Jehovah's Witnesses and Mormon proselytizers were required to spend two years attempting to convert *each other*, they would be less willing to seek converts thereafter, and they might even end up as religious relativists.

When we reflect on these facts, we realize that there is indeed a kind of deontological argument that can be directed against proselytizers and proselytizing. This deontological or Kantian argument can be understood on two levels. First, from a deontological standpoint, (attempted) proselytizing is only morally justifiable when the proselytizer is prepared to acknowledge *everyone's* right to proselytize by rational means. If a missionary is not prepared to acknowledge a universal right to proselytize by rational means, then he is rather narrow-minded, and his acts of (attempted) proselytizing are morally wrong on at least one level. But a person *can* acknowledge a universal right to proselytize in a way that he *cannot* acknowledge a universal right to break promises whenever it is expedient. Here it is important to recognize that the deontological argument can be understood on a *second* level. If everyone broke promises whenever he found it convenient to do so, the very institution of promising would collapse. What would happen in a society in which everyone was trying to proselytize everyone else? It is hard to say. Perhaps reason would prevail, and the best man would win. But perhaps a civil war, a holy war, would cause our imaginary society to collapse. Or perhaps people in this society would all come to regard proselytizing as silly and futile. In one way or other, the institution of proselytizing might well collapse in our imaginary society.

Our society is very different from the imaginary society that we have just considered. In our society, not everyone is interested in getting his fellow human beings to share his religious beliefs; many people are more interested in *learning* than in *persuading*. La Rochefoucauld observed with customary acuity that while many wish to be pious, few wish to be humble. But proselytizing continues to exist precisely because there are some people who are humble enough to be willing to allow others to attempt to convert them. In our imperfect society, some are obsessed with 'teaching,' others are obsessed with 'learning,' and few have found the proper balance between the two activities. One of the conditions of successful proselytizing is the receptivity of the potential convert. If everyone in our society was primarily a missionary and only secondarily a learner, this condition of receptivity would be lacking, and few people if any would be ripe for conversion. But we should not take La Rochefoucauld's judgment too seriously, especially in light of Nietzsche's equally profound insight that in the realm of religion there is a myriad of sheeplike followers for every charismatic leader.

As far as the deontologist is concerned, however, these psychological considerations are less important than genuine ethical considerations. The deontologist is not very concerned with the question of whether the relationship between the proselytizer and the potential convert is symbiotic or parasitic. Nor is the deontologist apt to be impressed when the proselytizer points out to him that no realist has to worry about what will happen when everyone tries to convert everyone else. To the deontologist, the fact that only certain people have an obsession with proselytizing is no more significant than the fact that only certain people are in the habit of breaking their promises whenever they find it expedient to do so.

It is not easy to determine how seriously the deontologist's argument should be taken. Pure deontologism appears to overemphasize duty at the expense of other ethical considerations, and it is especially difficult to determine how much importance to assign to conflicting deontological and utilitarian conclusions. Also, P_2 is likely to argue that only those who *know* which religious beliefs are true and good can proselytize by rational means, and since P_3's religious beliefs are not true or good, P_3 cannot possibly convert people by rational means and thus has no right to attempt to proselytize. P_2 may be quite willing to see everyone proselytize for P_2's faith even if he is adamantly opposed to everyone going out and proselytizing for one or another faith. A key weakness of Kantian deontologism is that it does not make clear to what particular kinds of practices it is appropriate to apply the test of universalizability.

EPISTEMOLOGICO-ETHICAL CONSIDERATIONS

This last point leads us to considerations involving the ethics of belief. A non-utilitarian, non-deontological philosopher can argue as follows: 'If x is true, then P has a moral right or even a moral obligation to get Q and others to believe x, even if their coming to believe x will lead to a *decrease* in the general happiness or P is unwilling to see other men proselytize in the way he does.' To most of us it is intuitively obvious that it is usually morally right to believe and also to teach *what is true*. But there are certain situations in which we consciously refrain from telling people the truth; for example, we do not go out of our way to tell a dying woman that her only son has been killed in an accident, and if she asks about her son's whereabouts, we may even lie and tell her that he cannot be with her because he is on some important patriotic mission. We all know that an educator has to be highly selective in presenting ideas to fragile young minds that are limited in their ability to grasp complex notions. Yet, we are rarely quick to condemn a person who acts on the principle that *no matter what the consequences*, he must believe and make known only that which appears to him to be true. In fact, we can admire such a person even though we disagree with him. But we can only admire him if he is a reasonable man who has good reasons for believing what he believes. Few are likely to respect a man who goes about trying to convince the world that the local government is run by creatures from outer space; it does not matter much that he is sincerely convinced that it is *true* that these creatures control the local government.

Now say that P argues that *no matter what the consequences*, he must, for moral reasons, attempt to get Q to believe what he, P, is firmly convinced is true. How are we to respond to such an argument? First, where possible, we should point out to P that in reality he is not as committed to this principle as he thinks he is (or is pretending he is). Rarely are proselytizers committed to making known the *whole* truth. Not only will few missionaries go out of their way to point out to a potential convert that, say, the missionary's co-religionists have at various times done some grossly immoral things (such as torturing heretics or excluding blacks from the clergy), but most missionaries *methodically conceal* truths because they feel that knowing some things is more important than knowing others. Some beliefs *are* more important than others; but if missionaries methodically conceal certain truths, they should not believe or pretend that they are wholly unconcerned with 'consequences.' We can respect a man who is both reasonable and frank; but it is harder to respect a man who, while claiming to be concerned above all with truth, tells many 'white' lies and systematically hides truths from us. Secondly, *when pertinent*, we should point out to P that if he does not have *good reasons* for believing x to be true, he may well be too casual in his approach to truth. Of course, if P *has* good reasons for believing x, and we cannot think of any better reasons for *not* believing x, this point is not pertinent.

Some people who know very little about religion mistakenly believe that religious or theological beliefs are never verifiable or falsifiable. Some religious beliefs are empirical and can be verified by reference to sense experience. If Q believes that sacrificing a virgin a week to some god makes the sun rise every day, a missionary can prove to him that this empirical religious belief is false. Also, historians have been able to verify some of the claims of the Bible. Whether or not there can also be synthetic a priori religious knowledge is, for me at least, an open question. In any case, as I mentioned earlier, I do believe that my most basic religious beliefs are more reasonable than alternative religious beliefs. Those who accept the fact of religious pluralism need not be committed to religious relativism. Religious pluralists do not have to be religious relativists in order to believe that the differences among the major religions are not so profound as to warrant taking the risk of greatly increasing tensions in the domain of religion, tensions that can easily spill over into all our social and political domains. It is one thing to disapprove of a man's religious beliefs; it is another to be willing to harass that man with bothersome proselytizing activities, especially at the risk of promoting social disunity, hatred, bitterness, and conditions of barbarism.

For most missionaries, the 'good news' that they wish to pass on is good because it is true. We must not make the mistake of thinking of missionaries as social workers who are primarily concerned with the physical well-being of savages and others; the missionary's main aim is to pass on the 'good news.' Christian missionaries (and most other Christians) have an attitude towards Christianity that precludes their seeing it as capable of being fitted into a neat synthesis with other major religions; it is purely a matter of speculation as to whether or not the world would be a better place if Christians, Moslems, and others had a different attitude towards their faith. But given their present attitude, most proselytizers, as we have seen, cannot be expected to have much interest in speculating about such utilitarian matters.

Underlying the question 'What right does P have to attempt to convert Q to belief in x?' is another question: 'What right does P have to believe x?' There are other underlying questions, but this one certainly cannot be ignored. Anyone who is concerned with problems of the ethics of belief has a great deal of interest in *evidence*. Here, however, we are not concerned with the arguments of the great philosophical theologians; we are concerned with ordinary missionary activity. Proselytizers often talk about evidence, but they are not as subtle as metaphysicians and epistemologists, and sooner or later most of them go back to talking about faith and revelation. From my own limited experience with proselytizers, it would appear that 1/proselytizers do not generally have compelling (or even good) reasons for believing x; 2 / proselytizers do not generally have a clear idea of what distinguishes good reasons for believing from bad ones; and 3 / the theories that proselytizers want men to believe are usually highly speculative, and I am not sure myself what would be the proper method for going about verifying or falsifying them.

Whether or not he is interested in utilitarian considerations, p almost surely thinks that he is doing something *for* q by changing q's religious beliefs. It is possible for a missionary to be willing to harm a potential convert for the good of the greatest number. But usually proselytizers believe that if they are not making the proselytes happier, they are at least making them better people by *some* standard. Even when heretics were about to be burnt at the stake, they were usually told that it was for their own good. Yet it is interesting that many who are anxious to share 'good news' are not eager to share much else. There are a few ascetic missionaries who are prepared to starve so that the children of savages can live; but usually not even these missionaries are anxious to help those who are firmly opposed to the missionaries' religious beliefs. The proselytizers who come to visit *me* seem to be prospering materially as well as emotionally, and I suspect that they are less liberal with their property and their money than they are with their theological reflections. I have occasionally had to resist the temptation to ask them, 'If you cannot save my soul, can you at least loan me a few dollars so that I can make it through the week-end?' My Marxist friends have suggested that 'good news' is a cheap commodity, at least as far as the seller is concerned; but they are more than a bit unfair. Proselytizers do sincerely believe that souls are important. The strange limitations of a missionary's goodwill do not in any way suggest that his religious doctrines are false or bad. They do suggest, perhaps, that he has not been reading the sacred books closely enough, for most works of religious literature conceive of charity rather broadly. They also suggest that he has much to learn as well as to teach.

We saw earlier that anyone who is opposed to radical ethical relativism believes that there is at least one ethical absolute and hence is committed in principle to appreciating the value of some ethical proselytizing. Since ethical proselytizing cannot be completely isolated from religious and metaphysical proselytizing, and since metaphysical relativism is itself an unacceptable position, the non-relativist is committed to appreciating the value of a limited amount of religious proselytizing. We also saw that there are probably many cases in which proselytizing is clearly conducive to an increase in the general happiness and hence, from a utilitarian standpoint, clearly morally right. But we could not help taking note of the fact that even from a utilitarian standpoint, most of the religious proselytizing that has gone on is probably morally unacceptable. Now that we have examined the relevant deontological and epistemologico-ethical considerations, we have also seen that none of them suggest that proselytizing in general is morally right, and some of them suggest that it is actually morally wrong. And so I think that we must conclude here that while a limited amount of religious proselytizing is morally advisable, most of the religious proselytizing that is going on in the world today is not even morally acceptable. One does not have to be a religious relativist to realize that there is a need in this area for restraint, for caution, much more than proselytizers have traditionally exhibited. The missionary is not excused from having to concern himself with trans-cultural ethical ideals; indeed these ideals are almost surely at the core of the faith that he is witnessing for.

Some will see my remarks as reflecting an untenable conservatism and irrationalism. They will argue that my views are those of a man who is opposed to *change* and *rational persuasion*. But I am no religious relativist, and I am not opposed to all proselytizing activity. I have argued that proselytizing is not necessarily immoral and have tried to show that under certain specific conditions it may even be morally advisable (for instance, when savages believe in a god who requires them to torture people). I have not even criticized the view that we should encourage change for its own sake, although surely *some* change should be discouraged. No matter what our views about truth, we can all see that persuading a person to be a Methodist or a Mormon is very different from persuading him that more people live in New York than in Toronto. Clearly there are times when persuasion is advisable and times when it is less advisable. So much conversation is argumentative and aims at persuasion; perhaps more should aim at the mutual enlightenment of the discussants. In his famous book *How to Win Friends and Influence People*, Dale Carnegie rightly observes that 'Nine times out of ten, an argument ends with each of the contestants being more firmly convinced than ever that he is absolutely right.' Moreover, 'You can't win an argument. You can't because if you lose it, you lose it; and if you win it, you lose it ... You have hurt [the other man's] pride. He will resent your triumph.'[3] We can win many arguments, but it is prudent and moral to resist the temptation to engage in rational persuasion at every opportunity. And since so much is at stake in religious arguments and disagreements, there is a need for special restraint in this area.

CONDITIONS OF RELIGIOUS DIALOGUE

In a pluralistic society, the main way in which people of different faiths come to co-operate and to be tolerant of one another is through religious dialogue. One of the most serious threats posed by the missionary is that he undermines people's confidence in the possibility of religious dialogue. If a man believes that men of other faiths simply want to convert him, not share in a constructive dialogue, he will eventually give up on ecumenical activities. Many religious leaders still confuse genuine religious dialogue with the missionary's monologue, a counterfeit article. The latter does not promote tolerance; if anything, as we have seen, it weakens it. Men of goodwill can only distinguish between the genuine article and the counterfeit one if they understand the conditions of religious dialogue.

Consider the teaching of Saint Thomas Aquinas in *Summa Theologiae*, ii–ii, q. 10, a. 7. If Aquinas is not the wisest or greatest of Christian philosophers, he has certainly been the most influential; so what he says about interfaith discussion is revealing. In the article in question, Saint Thomas considers whether Christians should enter into public debate with unbelievers.[4] He begins by listing three plausible objections: 1 / Saint Paul says (2 Timothy 2:14) that people should be warned not to dispute about words, for to do so is useless and only risks the ruination of the listeners. 2 / According to the law of Martianus Augustus, confirmed by the canons of the church, anyone who dares to reconsider and debate in public about matters that have been judged and disposed of by the church clearly insults the councils of the church. And 3 / debate involves *argument*, that is, reasoning to settle a matter in doubt; and since matters of faith are certain, they should not be debated about. Still, we are told in Acts 9:22 that Saul confounded the Jews with his proofs, and that he debated with the Greek-speaking Jews (9:29).

Accordingly, Aquinas makes these observations: 1 / Two sides must be considered in a debate, the speaker's and the listener's. If the speaker debated as though he had doubts about the faith, he would be sinning; but if he debates in order to refute errors, or as an exercise, he is praiseworthy.[5] With regard to the listener, much depends on whether or not he is firm in his faith. We do not have to worry about those who are wise and firm in their faith. But simple-minded listeners pose problems. If they are surrounded by Jews, heretics, or pagans who seek to corrupt their faith, they should be exposed to public debate, for then their faith will be strengthened, and infidels will be deprived of their ability to deceive. Simple-minded listeners who are not surrounded by infidels are better off not being exposed to public debate. 2 / The Apostle does not totally prohibit debates, only those that are inordinate and wordy.[6] The law prohibits public debate that arises from doubt about the faith, not that which aims at conserving the faith. 3 / We should debate about matters of faith in order to make the truth known and refute errors; such debating can defend the faith and convince those in error.[7] In the next article, Aquinas argues that heathens and Jews who have never received the faith should not be compelled to the faith in the way that heretics and apostates should; but they should be compelled not to hinder the faith by blasphemies or *evil persuasions*.[8] And in a. 9 Thomas argues that those who are firm in their faith may communicate with Jews and pagans, for through their communication they may convert the unbelievers. But simple-minded people should not be permitted to associate with Jews and pagans, for such communication can lead to their downfall; and communication with heretics and apostates is completely forbidden.

These passages from the *Summa Theologiae* represent the church's traditional position on the proper conditions of communication between Christians and outsiders. Under these conditions, the communication cannot qualify as dialogue. Dialogue requires the free interchange of ideas between two men who are both full-fledged speakers and full-fledged listeners. Under Aquinas's conditions, there can be non-religious dialogue between the Christian and the outsider, dialogue concerning, say, business matters. But there cannot be religious dialogue, and it is religious dialogue that represents our best opportunity for avoiding the ignorance that breeds intolerance and persecution. Consider these specific restrictions that Saint Thomas's church placed on communication between Christians and outsiders: 1 / The only Christians who may discuss religious matters with outsiders are those who will not be persuaded by any religious (or atheistic) argument that the outsider offers in defence of the reasonableness of his own faith. 2 / The religious arguments of outsiders are to be regarded as 'evil persuasions.' Accordingly, no contact between outsiders and simple-minded people is to be encouraged (or even permitted). 3 / Intelligent Christians have a moral obligation to engage in religious discussions with outsiders. But their principal motive should be to *convert* the unbelievers. Here, then, we have monologue rather than dialogue. The Christian has little interest in what the outsider has to say. The Christian who is firm in his faith is saying, in effect, 'I shall do the talking; you must listen; and if all goes well, you will come to see the truth.'

Saint Thomas draws our attention to an important question: What *motives* can a person have for entering into religious discussions with unbelievers or men of other faiths? Unfortunately, Thomas's own answer is superficial; like most religious leaders, he has failed to explore all the possibilities. His main problem here is that he is more concerned with the 'character' of the speakers than with the content of the discussion. He forces people into various categories; he tells us that there are wise Christians (firm in their faith), simple-minded Christians surrounded by outsiders, simple-minded Christians not surrounded by outsiders, Jews, pagans, heretics, and apostates. He then argues that the existence, nature, and purpose of religious discussion or disputation ought to depend on which of these categories the speaker and listener fit into. All of us, in our conversations, are guided to some extent by our perceptions of important qualities or character traits of the people with whom we speak. But we also realize that the soundness of arguments does not depend on the personality of the individual who advances them. The fact that a man is a Jew or a heretic does not in itself guarantee that his religious or anti-religious arguments are unworthy of consideration, or even that they are unsound. Indeed, if one were to reflect on the traditional use of the term 'dialogue,' one would probably conclude that one can only enter into dialogue if one has the courage of one's convictions and is prepared to expose one's own views to the test of critical scrutiny.

What kind of motives, then, does Aquinas ignore? One trivial one is the desire to be amused. We often find exotic ideas humorous, amusing. But surely the most important motives that he ignores are educational ones. The first of these is a practical one. If we are going to live in harmony with our neighbours, we ought to know something about their basic world-view. (If we are going to *love* our neighbours, we ought to know a great deal about their outlook.) Such practical knowledge is especially valuable in a society like ours, where the temporal power of churches is limited and there are important disagreements among numerous influential sects. Saint Thomas lived in a society that was dominated by a single powerful church, and so we should not be surprised that he took this practical educational motive for religious discussion so lightly.

There is a second practical educational motive for such discussion, and this one Aquinas should have been the last person to ignore. By talking with men of other faiths, by being prepared to learn from them, we can enrich our own faith. For one thing, the different religions have much in common. For another, outsiders often have access to sources of insight and information that are not available to us. Aquinas himself was not reluctant to borrow ideas from Jewish and Moslem philosophers. The author of the *Summa Theologiae* borrows proofs of God's existence from the Jewish Aristotelian Maimonides, and he speaks of the Arab Averroës as 'the Commentator' on Aristotle. Finally, there is a non-practical, 'intellectual' educational motive for religious communication. The world-view of an outsider is one of many things under the sun, and it must be understood by anyone who seeks a comprehensive vision of reality.

We know from its etymology that 'dialogue' is a talking *between* rather than a talking *at*. The evangelist, the missionary, the preacher are speaking *to* us, not *with* us. Aquinas believes that the public disputation between Christian and outsider should involve the former's speaking *to* the latter. In his eyes, the outsider has nothing to teach, and we should actually prevent the outsider from hindering the faith by 'evil persuasions.' Many pious Christians are motivated by a desire to make known the 'good news,' and they can appreciate Thomas's statement that Christians who are firm in their faith are morally obliged to enter into religious discussions with outsiders. But why should they ignore the educational value of genuine religious dialogue, especially when they can see that the most important of Christian philosophers has himself learned from the unbelievers?

The relationship between teacher and student rests on implicit trust. The student will only learn from the teacher if he is open, receptive. Saint Thomas is well aware of this fact, and that is why he wants to keep the simple-minded away from outsiders; he sees that the simple-minded are prepared to trust the judgment of 'persuasive' outsiders, that they are willing to be impressed. But in his view, the outsider should not be permitted to 'teach,' because the content of his doctrine is false, erroneous. Yet, the outsider's view of Christian doctrine is almost always the same. Most Jews, pagans, and atheists see Christian doctrine as riddled with confusions, superstitions, and falsehoods. Outsiders who are firm in their faith are basically no more receptive to proselytizing than Aquinas's 'wise' Christians are.

So these questions come to mind: 1 / If Jews and pagans should not be compelled to the faith, as Aquinas argues in a. 9, then to which people among them can the missionary be expected to appeal? Clearly the proselytizer's little speech will be most impressive to those who are simple-minded and not firm in their own faith. Aquinas believes that the Jew or pagan who is firm in his faith is not 'wise' in the way that the committed Christian is. But this point is certainly not obvious to the committed, reflective outsider. The reflective outsider is similar to the reflective Christian in that he can only be swayed by good reasons, good arguments. He may be receptive to the ideas of those who will talk *with* him, but he is not likely to be impressed by those who simply want to talk *to* him. Is it to the credit of the evangelist, the proselytizer, that his monologue appeals primarily to the simple-minded, ignorant, and unreflective? 2 / Is Aquinas's association of wisdom with firmness not perhaps misconceived? The best teachers are usually the best students. Willingness to learn from others is, with the ability to distinguish good arguments from sophistical ones, one of the basic conditions of intellectuality, the intellectuality that leads to wisdom. Are the committed Christian and the committed outsider truly wise or simply obstinate and dogmatic? 3 / Is the truth of any religious doctrine so *obvious* that acceptance of that doctrine should be allowed to be a determinant of the conditions of religious discussion? Most people in Saint Thomas's society were quite sure that the teachings of the Church of Rome are true. But there is not the same uniformity of religious opinion in our modern pluralistic society.

We have good reason to believe that Aquinas was considerably more enlightened in his views about outsiders than were most of his high-ranking co-religionists. Perhaps he himself had the courage of his convictions and was actually convinced that any reflective Christian can successfully defend the faith in public disputations. But it is a historical fact worth reflecting upon that those medieval Christian leaders who shared Thomas's belief in the importance of public 'debate' were not interested in serious disputation. Medieval religious 'debates' were invariably side-shows at best and often examples of sophistical deception or even brute compulsion. Starting with Aquinas's premise that the main object of religious discussion is to convert the infidel, church leaders quickly abandoned dialogue in favour of more repressive forms of communication:

In 1263, a new tactical experiment was tried, pressure being exerted on the Aragonese communities [of Jews] by staging a public disputation at Barcelona in the presence of the king, at which the apostate friar Pablo Christiani pitted himself against the learned Rabbi Moses ben Nahman ('Ramban' or Nahmanides, 1194–1270). Though the latter more than held his own, this was followed by an attempt to suppress the study of the talmudic literature and to compel the Jews to offer the hospitality of their synagogues for the delivery of conversionist sermons. In 1280, the Jews of Castile were arrested and thrown into prison.[9]

We cannot blame Saint Thomas for the stupidity of his fanatic co-religionists; but we can lament the fact that he drew the attention of many of them to the *conversionist* value of religious communication rather than the *educational* value.

What, then, are the conditions of genuine religious dialogue? We should not find it hard to answer this question as long as we remember that religious dialogue is *both* a kind of religious communication and a kind of dialogue. When a Roman Catholic and a Presbyterian discuss ordinary business matters, they are not engaged in religious dialogue, except perhaps when their business concerns and their religious concerns overlap; so, obviously, one condition of religious dialogue is that it deal directly with religious matters. The other condition of religious dialogue, the one involving dialogue, is less obvious. Religious dialogue, or any other form of dialogue, requiring as it does a talking *between* rather than a talking *at*, requires that those who enter into it be full-fledged, sincere *listeners* as well as full-fledged, sincere *speakers*, that they be prepared to learn as well as to teach. In effect, it requires that one respect the integrity and rationality of one's partner in discussion. (It does not, of course, require that one believe that this man's beliefs are as true or as good as one's own.) Those who are not willing to make this commitment may be effective missionaries or 'witnesses,' but they are not capable of entering into religious dialogue.

I am not arguing here that religious dialogue is the only wholesome form of religious communication. I think it important, however, that we distinguish conversionist motives for engaging in interfaith discussion from more profound motives. Most religious proselytizing tends to promote resentment. Resentment promotes intolerance, which in turn promotes barbarism. But religious dialogue tends to promote understanding. Understanding promotes tolerance, which in turn promotes civilization.

6

Exclusivism and universalism

The Roman church conceives of itself as a Catholic institution, 'catholic' in the sense of universal. Those who worship in the Roman church believe that the church is the mystical Body of Christ, the bride of Christ, the kingdom of God begun here on earth; and they look forward to the time when all men will be united in the church. The church is not 'catholic' in fact; most people in the world do not believe in the teachings of popes and bishops and priests. Rather, it is 'catholic' in that it strives to be universal, in that it seeks to incorporate all human beings. In the Middle Ages, this aim was not as unrealistic as it is now. In our day and age, all of the well-known religious bodies are catholic in intent, for all of them seek to bring all human beings over to their side, into their own religious community, over to their way of seeing things. Because they are catholic or universalistic in this way, all well-known religious bodies seek in one way or other to make converts. Every church has its propagandists, missionaries, and philosophers, and every church teaches that its members should see themselves as 'witnesses.'

But religious bodies have always differed dramatically in their approach to the obligation to witness. Many people associate Islam and medieval Christianity with the most militant, aggressive, and forceful methods of making converts: threats, deception, violence, forced conversion, holy war. Many people who think of the Mormons or Jehovah's Witnesses immediately think of their unusually annoying proselytizing methods. Southern Baptists are often judged by the behaviour of slick television evangelists. Liberals are quick to condemn the Roman Catholic church for its extraordinarily sophisticated methods of moulding minds and bringing about the evangelization of peoples. Other religious groups are associated with a 'soft sell.' Most Methodists and Presbyterians are repelled by the proselytizing methods of Mormons and Catholics. Yet they too, in their own subtle way, work slowly towards fulfilling their own universalistic aspirations. But without a doubt, the softest sell of all is that of the Jews, and this fact is one that bears much reflecting upon.

It is well known that the Jews have rarely sought to make converts in an active way. Yet Judaism is, along with ancient Greek humanism, the fountainhead of all western religion and spirituality, indeed of all western civilization. The Jews are the descendants of the first great moral teachers in western history; even most of their persecutors have acknowledged that their own morality and faith have Jewish roots. And in spite of countless efforts to wipe them out, the Jews have always played a mysteriously significant and conspicuous role in the unfolding of human destiny. Yet, though they have tried to check assimilation and apostasy, Jewish leaders have rarely made a serious attempt at proselytizing on a large scale.

A widespread and inadequate explanation of this phenomenon is that Judaism is essentially a tribal or group religion, that is, that unlike Christians and Moslems, Jews are religious exclusivists rather than religious universalists. But as we shall now see, the great Jewish leaders and teachers have tried to blend exclusivistic and universalistic elements in such a way as to produce and maintain a conception of the role of the Jew in the world which is conducive to both strong moral commitment and a spirit of religious tolerance.

EXCLUSIVISM AND UNIVERSALISM IN JUDAISM

According to the Russian Orthodox philosopher Nicolas Berdyaev, Judaism is a form of racism. (This view is echoed in many contemporary attacks on Zionism.) With one eye on Hitlerism and Nazi atrocities, Berdyaev writes:

Racialism is a purely Hebrew ideology. The only classic example in history of the racialist ideal is that afforded by the Jews. It was the Jewish race which strove for racial purity, opposed mixed marriages and all sorts of mingling with others, strove to remain a world closed to outsiders. Judaism gave religious significance to blood-relationship and bound up inseparably the religious element with that of Nationalism. The Messianic consciousness of any people is always an evidence of the Jewish spirit. Exclusiveness, the loyalty to one's own things and people only, is one of the prime qualities of Judaism. Thus the anti-Semite may well be accused of Jewish practice and spirit. It is just we non-Jews who should be far from all racialism, exclusive Nationalism, all Messianism. Such 'Aryan' groups as the Hindus or the Greeks are more naturally individualists, in the ancient, rather than the modern meaning of that word. They set more value upon soul, spirit, bodily form, than upon the fate of the national collective. Fanaticism, intolerance or exclusiveness are not character-istic traits of these groups.[1]

Berdyaev associates tolerance with universalism, intolerance with exclusivism. (On this point, and probably this one only, his theory of religious intolerance is in agreement with Allport's.) Berdyaev has failed to understand the negative side of religious universalism, and this failure, combined with his lack of insight into the universalistic aspects of Judaism, has led him to a ridiculous 'rationalization' of his anti-Semitism.

There is no mention of 'race' or 'races' in the Torah, Prophets, Writings, Midrash, Mishnah, Gemara, *Moreh Nebuchim*, *Kuzari*, or any other work to which Jews have traditionally turned in their search for wisdom. The genuine Jewish concept that is relevant here is that of the 'children of Israel' or the 'Jewish people'; this concept is ambiguous, open-ended, and anyone who has made a serious effort to understand the sacred literature of the Jews knows that it always was. Moses himself married a daughter of the priest of Midian (Exodus 2:15–22), who later converted to his son-in-law's faith (Numbers 10:29–32). At various times in their history the Jews have actively sought proselytes; but at all times in their history it has been their hope that all peoples will embrace the way of Torah (cf., for instance, Isaiah 2:3, 42:6, 60:3). Jewish opposition to mixed marriages and ethnic assimilation has traditionally been based on a concern for the survival of Jewish ideology and spirituality. It has been most conspicuous in periods when Jews have perceived their world-view and way of life as threatened. There has always been a mechanism of (what is now called) 'conversion' in Judaism, although it has rarely been applied as promiscuously as similar mechanisms have been applied among most Christian groups.

'Racialism' is rooted in tribalism, which is in turn rooted in the institution of the family. One of the earliest insights of the Torah is that we are our brother's keeper (Genesis 4:9–11); the concept of brother-hood here is again ambiguous, open-ended, but significant. Berdyaev's talk about 'spiritual individualism' is naïve. We all know what it is to have a special concern for a loved one – parent, child, teacher, or friend

– who does not share our ideology. One does not have the same love for strangers that one has for one's parents, even if the strangers share one's religious and political opinions while one's parents do not. There is an element of 'exclusiveness' in love for one's parents, children, and others. It protects us from both egoism and alienation. But this kind of love is not the only love of which human beings are capable. They are also capable of loving their fellow man, who is also a 'brother' of sorts.

The ancient Israelites transcended the narrow tribalism of the peoples surrounding them; their metaphysical monotheism was itself a repudiation of tribalism, tribal deities, and tribal codes. Certainly Judaism contains at least the seed of universalism. It speaks of one God who loves all men, and it teaches that all men, regardless of their tribe, have certain rights as human beings. And so it is absurd to say that 'racialism' is a purely Hebrew ideology. Blood-relationship was an important consideration in pre-Israelite cultures, and it is an important consideration in societies like our own. It has been an important consideration in every community where the family or the tribe has been a major institution. However, as a repudiation of narrow tribalism, Judaism represents an attack on the *roots* of 'racialism.'

The element of 'exclusiveness' in Judaism must never be understood in terms of a refusal to consider the rights and interests of outsiders (again see Exodus 23:9). It is true that Judaism fosters a 'loyalty to one's own things only'; but this 'exclusiveness' amounts to a recognition of the fact that one cannot simultaneously be a Jew and a pagan. Jews are no relativists. One cannot simultaneously believe in one God and worship idols. One cannot simultaneously follow the ethical way of Torah and indulge in human sacrifice, theft, and adultery. Alas, few peoples, including the Christian peoples, have treated the Jews with as much dignity as the Jews have treated outsiders. For even when the Jews have sought to isolate themselves and their culture from strangers and strange influences, they have rarely gone out of their way to harm other peoples or interfere destructively with their ways of life. So the anti-Semite can hardly be seen as conforming to Jewish practice and spirit.

If one regards ideological 'exclusiveness' as a commitment to the view that one's own religious beliefs are true or reasonable in a way that alternative religious beliefs are not, then the alternative to ideological 'exclusiveness' is clearly relativism. Judaism, Christianity, and the philosophies of 'Aryan' groups are genuine alternatives, for though they share certain fundamental metaphysical and ethical principles, they are significantly different from one another in content and emphasis. Perhaps one can simultaneously admire all of them. Certainly one can tolerate those who practise them. But one cannot simultaneously be committed to all of them. Though opposed to fanaticism, intolerance, and some form of 'exclusiveness,' Berdyaev himself is sophisticated enough to realize, as some advocates of the ecumenical spirit do not, that the ancient religious conflict between Christianity and Judaism has been a real one.[2] But then ideological 'exclusiveness' works both ways: the true Christian is as committed to Christianity as the true Jew is to Judaism. The committed Christian cannot accept Judaism as the true or best religion any more than the committed Jew can accept Christianity as the true or best religion. Even those eastern religions that incorporate elements of syncretism are not completely compatible with Judaism, Christianity, Islam, or even each other.

It is worth reflecting on the fact that Christian persecution of the Jews has been one of the dominant themes of western religious history. As Father Edward Synan has observed, 'Europe dominated by the papacy, it can be argued, knew neither equality nor justice; medieval legislation was as savage in its intentions as in its penalties, and the brunt of these fell upon the helpless Jewish population. The medieval Jew went in fear of mob violence, a threat often tolerated and, at times, incited by the authorities responsible for public order. Badge and ghetto sealed with humiliation a systematic drive to degrade the whole Jewish community.'[3] Nor is this persecution a thing of the past, for as Synan points out, 'not all Christians reach the standard set by Pope John XXIII. In his country club and neighborhood, in some rectories, kinship according to the flesh with the Nazarene all Christians call their Lord does not count necessarily as a patent of nobility.'[4] If Jews have not persecuted Christians to the same extent, it may well be simply because the Jews have not had the numbers or the power of the Christians among whom they have lived. We shall never know. But take note of the fact that the worst religious fanaticism and intolerance that the world has known has been a product of a 'universalistic' or 'catholic' outlook.

Jews have traditionally accepted the fact that most men do not share their religious philosophy. They have had to be tolerant; they have had no other choice. But they have rarely even bothered to proselytize in an aggressive way. Again, Jews cannot afford to be as aggressive or militant as the Christians, Moslems, or atheists among whom they live. But Jews have not even encouraged potential proselytes who have expressed an interest in embracing Judaism. The rabbis warn that the Jewish way of life is not an easy one; in addition to worrying about persecution, the Jew must observe hundreds of commandments set out in the Torah. It is hard to be a Jew; why, they ask the potential proselyte, are you so anxious to embrace a way of life that is so demanding? Only when they are positively convinced that the potential proselyte thoroughly understands the complexity of a commitment to the Jewish way of life and the Jewish way of viewing the world will the orthodox rabbis welcome him into the fold. Moreover, the committed Jew does think of himself as a witness. Strangers can read the sacred books for themselves and judge for themselves what is of value in the Jewish religion. But *this* kind of 'exclusiveness' does not characterize the militantly universalistic religious groups. Most Christian leaders are not willing to wait for potential proselytes to come to Christianity; they believe that Christianity must be *brought* to the peoples of the world. The 'good news' must be proclaimed throughout the world (Matthew 24:14). And so the 'fanatic,' 'intolerant,' 'exclusive' Jews have been dragged before proselytizers and propagandists, and when they have proved to be too 'fanatic' and recalcitrant, they have been ridiculed, vilified, prevented from practising their religion, and even tortured and killed.

For the most part, the Jews have successfully steered a middle course between the Scylla of relativism and the Charybdis of intolerance. Judaism would not have survived through the millennia if the Jews had believed that the teachings of the Torah and the Prophets and the rabbis are no better than the teachings of pagans, Christians, Moslems, and materialists. And yet the Jews have tended to be, for pragmatic and philosophical reasons, reluctant to proselytize aggressively and risk angering their gentile neighbours. They have not hidden the ideals and teachings of the Torah. What people has provided more in the way of moral and spiritual education than this 'exclusive' people? If Jewish 'exclusiveness' amounts to a refusal to proselytize aggressively, perhaps the more universalistic churches should aim at being somewhat more 'exclusive.' Then we would be spared the fanaticism and intolerance of future generations of Crusaders and Inquisitors. As for the social 'exclusiveness' of the Jews, its origins are not difficult to understand. This kind of 'exclusiveness' has been a natural reaction to attempts to destroy their culture, world-view, and way of life. In any case, it was not the Jews who created the ghetto but the gentiles, and when the walls of the ghetto have been broken down, Jews have usually blended into the society at large rather quickly, often too quickly for their own good.

At the time when Berdyaev wrote the passage that we have been considering, many people were frightened by the word 'nationalism' because they associated it with the totalitarianism of Hitler's national socialism and Mussolini's corporate state. The power of the nation is ultimately derived from the individuals who compose it, and so in an important sense it is derived at the expense of other social institutions: smaller institutions (for instance, the family, the club, the town, the province), large institutions (international churches, fraternal orders, labour organizations), and instruments of world government (the United Nations and the International Court of Justice). The power of the nation is also derived at the expense of the individual, although in theory the individual gives up personal rights only so that he can enjoy the benefits that come from belonging to a nation-state. So we should not be surprised by the frequency with which the power of the nation is criticized. Many conservatives resent paying taxes to help support the poor; communists see nationalism as a threat to world communist government; some people object to having their schools racially integrated; and large ecclesiastical institutions see nationalism as a major force promoting secularism.

Now, nationalism can be good or bad. It is good when national aspirations are healthy and progressive; it is bad when national aspirations reflect a callousness, materialism, jealousy, and ignorance. It is not clear whether over the centuries human organization into national groups has promoted more justice than injustice, more progress than reaction. But if national power can be put to bad use, so can the power of an individual (for instance, a rapist or sniper), a fraternal order (the Ku Klux Klan), a church (as in the Inquisition), or an international organization (as when troops from several eastern European nations invaded Czechoslovakia). Civilization continues only because the power of individuals and social groups can be curbed. Nations often have to be curbed; but often they have to do the curbing too. In a healthy nation, national power is used to protect the citizens, not harm them; it is used to protect them from each other as well as from outsiders.

If there is nothing wrong with the nationalism *as such*, then Berdyaev either is terribly confused or believes that Jewish nationalism is particularly bad, reactionary, and harmful. If Berdyaev holds this belief, then in having articulated it he owes us something in the way of a rational defence of it. I do not envy anyone who hopes to defend it; for who can avoid being impressed by the stability and spirituality of a nation-state that, though surrounded by paganism and barbarism and materialism, has been guided by the Ten Commandments and the ethical precepts of the Pentateuch? Judaism has, as Berdyaev rightly observes, bound up inseparably the religious element with that of nationalism. Berdyaev interprets this phenomenon in terms of a deplorable 'exclusiveness,' and he fails to see its real significance. The ancient Israelites realized that the unity of the children of Israel should *not* depend solely on race, location, language, and other purely physical or external attributes; they saw the key to Jewish unity and Jewish destiny to be something spiritual and ideological – a sound philosophy. For this reason, descendants of the ancient Israelites cannot accept Berdyaev's dichotomy of soul/spirit vs the fate of the national collective. The fate of the Jewish people is bound up inseparably with the ideals of Judaism; and, of course, the Messianic consciousness of the Jewish people can only be understood by those who have grasped this point.

Modern Jews resemble their earliest spiritual ancestors in many ways, and certainly they can be stiff-necked and bigoted. Yet, of all the groups in our society, none is more identified with liberal attitudes than the Jewish people. We can see that Jewish liberalism is rooted partly in the reflection of Jews on their own sufferings at the hands of fanatics and bigots. We should also consider, however, the interesting mixture of exclusivistic and universalistic elements in the Jewish religion, for it not only explains certain aspects of Jewish liberalism but also reminds us of an important dimension of the problem of religious intolerance, the destructive force of unbounded universalism.

THE DOCTRINE OF EXCLUSIVE SALVATION

In our analysis of Berdyaev's talk about Jewish 'exclusiveness,' we saw that religious exclusivism may involve a number of things, and then we were only scratching the surface, for there are as many forms of religious exclusivism as there are ways of using the word 'only' when talking about religions. Berdyaev thought of exclusivism/universalism as a matter of how many people are encouraged to join the community of believers. The Jews are exclusivists, he felt, because they place 'racial' and 'nationalistic' restrictions on what kinds of people can be brought within the fold. His theory is inadequate, as we have seen, for a variety of reasons; but perhaps the most important weakness in the theory is its failure to recognize that one form of religious exclusivism may be necessary for the avoidance of a more dangerous form. All the well-known western religions are exclusivistic in holding themselves up as the true and / or best religion. All are exclusivistic in aiming to draw people away from the 'competition.' Berdyaev seems to believe that only those churches that use a 'hard sell' – that is, that proselytize aggressively – are truly universalistic and tolerant. But if the Jehovah's Witness is tolerant in genuinely wanting to bring all men into the fold as quickly as possible, he is intolerant in being unable to accept the fact of religious pluralism. He is a religious universalist in one sense but a religious exclusivist in another: he wants to bring *all* men into *his particular* community of believers. Since Berdyaev has not grasped this point, he cannot explain why the worst intolerance and persecution has always come from the churches *he* defines as universalistic and tolerant.

Let us consider now a related form of religious exclusivism, one that can be summarized by the slogan 'No salvation outside the church.' A man is certainly a religious exclusivist in one sense if he believes that the only people who will be saved are those who join his church. A typical exponent of this kind of religious exclusivism was Nicholas Wiseman, one of the most important of all English Catholic leaders. In his published lectures of 1835, Wiseman defends the Catholic rule of faith and argues against what he perceives as English anti-Catholic prejudice. In listing the reasons for hostility to Catholicism, Wiseman singles out one as being of special importance: 'I mean that doctrine which is known by the almost odious appellation of *exclusive salvation.* This is considered the harshest, the most intolerable point of the Catholic creed, touching its rule of faith; that we hold ourselves so exclusively in possession of God's truth, as to consider all others essentially in error, and not to allow that, through their belief, salvation is to be obtained.'[5] Wiseman's defence is far from conciliatory:

Upon this matter, allow me to observe, in the first place, that you will find it difficult to analyze, to its extreme consequences, the principle of any church professing to have a code or rule of faith, without finding yourselves led to the implicit maintenance of some such doctrine as this. When a church draws up a confession of faith, and commands all to sign and submit to it, and proclaims that eternal punishment will reach all who refuse, assuredly it supposes that the teaching of such doctrines is issentially [sic] necessary to salvation. If not, what constitutes the necessity of doctrine in reference to the revelation from God? Our Saviour comes down from heaven, on purpose to teach mankind; does he propose his doctrines under a penalty or not? Does he say, you may receive or reject these as you please? If not, is there not something incurred by refusing to accept them? Is there not the displeasure and indignation of God? (p. 271)

For Wiseman, these questions are hypothetical; anyone who reflects on them, he feels, will recognize that 'consequently, a penalty is necessarily affixed to the refusal of those obligations which Christ considered essential to faith' (p. 271). But has Wiseman weighed the alternatives?

The central theme of Wiseman's defence is a theoretical one: in any serious religion (that is, 'any church professing to have a code or rule of faith'), there *must* be at least the implicit maintenance of some doctrine like the Roman Catholic doctrine of exclusive salvation. Is this theory consistent with empirical data? Wiseman thinks so and directs our attention to the eighteenth of the thirty-nine articles of Anglicanism:

Looking, for instance, at the formulary of the Church of England, contained in the Athanasian creed, and appointed to be read in churches, I would ask if it be possible for any man of common understanding, to read its commencement and conclusion, and not be satisfied that its meaning is, that whoever does not believe the dogmas contained in it, is out of the way of salvation? ... It is, therefore, most unjust to condemn the Catholic church for holding only the same doctrine as is taught by others (p. 272).

These remarks are disturbing for several reasons. I am no authority on Anglican theology, and I have little interest in the theological disputes between the Church of England and the Church of Rome. But as an outsider I have been able to detect certain distinctions in doctrinal *emphasis*. The Church of England does not consider itself a 'catholic' church in quite the same way as the Church of Romes does. Perhaps this is the main reason why, as Wiseman himself notes, the missionary zeal of Anglican proselytizers is somewhat weaker than that of Roman Catholic proselytizers (pp. 133–216). We must not ignore the Protestant or evangelical aspects of Anglicanism. The average Anglican church-goer does not seem to have the same obsession with exclusive salvation as the average Catholic. And though it is valuable to take a hard look at the eighteenth article, we should be very careful before drawing the conclusion that the average Anglican churchgoer is a hypocrite. It is hard to believe that so many intelligent Anglicans subscribe to a doctrine that they are so critical of others for holding.

In any case, this question is a theological one that I am not intellectually equipped to handle. But let us assume, for the sake of argument, that Wiseman is right here. So what? At one level we can interpret Wiseman's argument as a case of the informal fallacy of *tu quoque*. From the fact that the Anglican theologian makes the same error in judgment as the Catholic theologian, it in no way *follows* that the Anglican theologian's criticism of that error is unjustified. Wiseman has a right (and a responsibility) to deplore Anglican prejudice against Catholics even though Wiseman's own church has persecuted non-Catholics for centuries. The rightness or wrongness of prejudice and persecution does not depend on the integrity of those who are arguing about it; it only depends on the soundness of relevant arguments. Similarly, the rightness or wrongness of the doctrine of exclusive salvation does not depend on the integrity of those who are arguing about it; even hypocrites are capable of presenting sound criticisms of doctrines which they themselves hold on one level.

But again assuming, for the sake of argument, that Wiseman's interpretation of Anglican theology is correct here, can we generalize from this one datum? Of all the religions of the world, Anglicanism is the one closest to Catholicism in doctrine and spirit. But do all Protestant churches believe in some kind of exclusive salvation? Does the Jewish community? Does the Buddhist community? Wiseman is committed to the view that either they believe in 'some such doctrine as this' or they do not constitute churches that profess to have a code or rule of faith.

Wiseman is dabbling here in the area of comparative religion, but he has not done his homework. Consider the case of the Jews. In his third lecture, Wiseman writes:

You are doubtless aware that a divine and bishop of the established church (Warburton) wrote a very erudite treatise, to prove the divine legation of Moses, on the extraordinary ground that he was able to achieve the great work of organizing a republic, and constituting a law to bind the people, without the sanction of a future state. He maintains with the strongest arguments, and the greatest show of plausibility, that you cannot discover in the writings of Moses, or of the earlier Jews, one single positive text in proof of the future existence of the soul, or of a place of rewards and punishments in another life ... But yet did the Jews believe in them? Did they possess them? Assuredly they did. For it is manifest from many passages of the New Testament and from their own works, that the doctrines of a future state and a resurrection were fully believed and taught ... So true is this, that the Sadducees, followed in later times by the Karaites, formed a sect among the Jews, who rejected the traditional doctrines, and consequently the resurrection of the dead, and the existence of a spiritual soul in men. (pp. 60–1)

By referring to the Sadducees and the Karaites, Wiseman has himself supplied counter-examples to his theory that in any serious religion there must be at least the implicit maintenance of some doctrine of exclusive salvation. Wiseman has also acknowledged the fact that Warburton has made his important point 'with the strongest arguments, and the greatest show of plausibility.' But we must also question Wiseman's thesis that the early Jews 'traditionally' believed in some form of exclusive salvation.

Jewish eschatology underwent much development over the centuries; Maimonides has much to say about the resurrection of the dead, the immortality of the soul, and the world to come. But what was pre-Pharisaic eschatology like? It is helpful to consider these observations of the eminent Jewish scholar Louis Finkelstein:

> The expectation that the struggles of the world would culminate in a glorious Messianic Age, ushering in peace and tranquility reminiscent of Adam's Paradise, had long been prominent in Israel's thought; and this offered an excellent background for the new faith. Several passages in the Second Isaiah seem to indicate that already he had been thinking in terms of the resurrection; but it remained for a later prophet, the author of Isaiah, chapters 24–27, to avow the belief clearly and explicitly. ...
>
> But this doctrine had been so long and so pointedly ignored among the Jews that the introduction of it might well have appeared to be defection to foreign worship. Moreover, appealing as a future life might seem, the belief in it was derived from animism, ancestor worship, and other primitive errors which were hated and despised by the Jewish religious teachers. Throughout the duration of the First Commonwealth they had struggled against its infiltration from Egypt and had on the whole succeeded in keeping Jewish faith free from the taint both of the resurrection and of the superstitions associated with it.[6]

When belief in a 'world to come' did become popular among the Jews, it was not the kind of belief that Wiseman has in mind; for it was then widely held that though the wicked of Israel are judged according to their transgressions, they still have a share in the world to come. And the Talmud states quite explicitly that the pious of *all* nations have a share in the world to come.

Consider also the principles of Calvinism. In the *Institutes*, Calvin writes: 'As Scripture, then, clearly shows, we say that God once established by his eternal and unchangeable plan those whom he long before determined once for all to receive into salvation, and those whom, on the other hand, he would devote to destruction. We assert

123 Exclusivism and universalism

that, with respect to the elect, this plan was founded upon his freely given mercy, without regard to human worth; but by his just and irreprehensible but incomprehensible judgment he has barred the door of life to those whom he has given over to damnation.'[7] Those who assign some place in election to works, Calvin argues, 'evade the apostle's contention that the distinction between the brothers [Jacob and Esau] depends not upon any basis of works but upon the mere calling of God, because it was established between them before they were born.'[8] And Calvin, of course, presents many more arguments in defence of his intepretation of Scripture. The details of the dispute between Roman Catholic and Calvinist theologians do not concern us here. But we should take note of the fact that some churches do not hold the same kind of doctrine of exclusive salvation as is taught by the Roman church. Calvinists, for example, believe that only certain people are saved; yet, their conception of election is such that it cannot serve the purpose for which Wiseman thinks a doctrine of exclusive salvation is necessary. There is obviously a disagreement here about what 'constitutes the necessity of doctrine in reference to the revelation from God.'

We must distinguish between the doctrine of exclusive salvation and the doctrine of exclusive possession of God's truth. These are two different forms of religious exclusivism. Certainly the latter is a central doctrine of most religions, although there is an important element of syncretism in some of the eastern religions. In any case, in some important religions, the 'necessity of doctrine in reference to the revelation from God' has little or nothing to do with the desire for salvation (or at least the kind of salvation of which Wiseman is speaking). We have also seen that some religious leaders believe that salvation is not as 'exclusive' as Wiseman thinks it must be. So we have disposed of the central theme of Wiseman's defence.

But though we have dealt with an important *empirical* question, we have not as yet considered the interesting philosophical question that Wiseman has raised in defence of the doctrine of exclusive salvation: 'If not [the doctrine of exclusive salvation], what constitutes the necessity of doctrine in reference to the revelation from God?' Consider again Wiseman's list of hypothetical questions: 'Our Saviour comes down from heaven, on purpose to teach mankind; does he propose his doctrines under a penalty or not?' Surely we must answer this question in the affirmative; but if the penalty is not exclusive destruction, what can it be? 'Does he say, you may receive or reject these [doctrines] as you please?' In a sense, if men have free will, then they may receive or reject doctrines as they please, and they do. But a saviour or prophet tries hard to teach men what he thinks they *ought* to believe, and surely he holds that they will be better off if they do believe these things. And so we must again give an affirmative answer to Wiseman's question. 'Is there not something incurred by refusing to accept them?' Perhaps there is even what Wiseman describes as 'the displeasure and indignation of God,' although a good many intelligent people have trouble conceiving of the highest of all beings as being pleased, displeased, or indignant. The question that we are left with, then, comes to this: What is the penalty for disobeying a prophet, and what is the reward for obeying him?

For the humanistic rationalist, this question must be translated into the *ethical* question: 'Why should we be moral?' This philosophical question is a very familiar one, and there is no dearth of philosophical answers to it. Even religious philosophers sometimes insist that we translate the religious question into a purely ethical one. For example, in the *Republic* (367e), Plato has Adimantus make an interesting request of Socrates: 'Do not, then, I repeat, merely prove to us in argument the superiority of justice to injustice, but show us what it is that each inherently does to its possessor – whether he does or does not escape the eyes of gods and men – whereby the one is good and the other evil.'[9] Plato is certainly not denying the existence of the gods, nor is he even denying that the gods will reward the just; he is simply having Adimantus ask why it pays to be moral even when the gods are not watching. Spinoza is less conciliatory. After the young Catholic bigot Albert Burgh begged him 'not to continue to pervert others' and to avoid 'eternal damnation' by following him into the Roman Catholic church, Spinoza wrote back, 'Your letter clearly shows that you have become a slave of this Church, under the influence not so much of the love of God as of the fear of hell, which is the sole cause of superstition.'[10] A decade earlier, Spinoza had touched upon the subject of salvation in a letter to Blyenbergh:

However, in answer to the first question I say that Scripture, since it especially serves the common people, continually speaks in human fashion, for the people are not capable of understanding high matters. And therefore, I believe that all those things which God revealed to the prophets as necessary to salvation, are written in the form of laws ... Salvation and perdition, which are no more than the effects which necessarily follow from these means, they represented as reward and punishment. And they adapted all their words to this parable rather than to the truth. And everywhere they described God as a man, now angry, now merciful, now desiring the future, now seized by jealousy and suspicion, and even deceived by the Devil. So that Philosophers, and with them all those who are above the Law, that is, who follow virtue not as a Law but from love of it because it is the best thing, need not trouble about such words.[11]

Spinoza clearly considers himself anything but an atheist; he sees himself as a man who loves, but has no reason to fear, God. His philosophical idea of 'salvation' is very different from that of Burgh, Wiseman, and others who are not capable of understanding 'high matters.' But even though Spinoza believes that we should strive for something that he occasionally calls 'salvation,' many religious people are likely to feel that Spinoza is being dishonest in calling it by this name, feigning orthodoxy and capitalizing on the emotive force of the word 'salvation' by attaching it to something he is trying to promote.

Still, if one believes that men are saved because of what they *do* (as opposed to what they *believe* about ultimate reality), then it is not hard to see salvation as something that is not as 'exclusive' as Wiseman thinks it is. Since different ways of life can be based on the same *general* approach to realizing trans-cultural ideals, there may be alternative routes to salvation. And even if believing the truth is one such route, there may still be others. Colerus tells the following little anecdote about Spinoza: 'It happened one day that his Landlady ask'd him whether he believed she cou'd be saved in the Religion she profest: He answered, *Your religion is a good one; you need not look for another, nor doubt that you may be saved in it, provided, whilst you apply your self to Piety, you live at the same time a peaceable and quiet life.*'[12] And when Burgh told Spinoza that he staked on his philosophy not only his peace of mind but the eternal salvation of his soul, Spinoza replied: 'You will, however, be unable to deny, unless perhaps you have lost your memory with your reason, that in every Church there are many very honest men who worship God with justice and charity ... Therefore you must allow that holiness of life is not peculiar to the Roman Church, but is common to all.'[13]

To such liberal statements a Wiseman must reply either that the most important moral values are uniquely Roman Catholic values or that salvation depends at least partly on what one believes about ultimate reality rather than wholly on what one does. A Wiseman could use passages from the New Testament to build a case for both of these positions. Other passages (for instance, 1 Corinthians 12:1–11) could be used to support a more liberal position. Biblical theologians must decide which position has the soundest scriptural basis. But which has the soundest philosophical basis? Certainly it is at least philosophically *plausible* that God is more impressed by actions than beliefs; or he may be impressed by some combination of actions and beliefs. But even if God is mainly or exclusively concerned with our metaphysical beliefs, it still does not follow that there is only one religion that guarantees salvation. The creeds of the Catholic, Lutheran, Jew, and Moslem are not completely consistent, and Catholics, Lutherans et al. cannot all be in complete possession of a perfectly true doctrine. But perhaps God is more impressed with the beliefs that they share than with the beliefs that only some of them hold. Even false beliefs might be acceptable to God; an honest doubter with a few intelligent insights may impress God more than a smug, unreflective, uncreative believer.

Wiseman is right in believing that the fear of hell (or desire for some reward) leads many men to be scrupulous in their religious observances. But there are a good many religious people whose religious commitments are based on loftier considerations: love of God, belief in divine wisdom, philosophical arguments, and so forth. In short, the doctrine of exclusive salvation is not a necessary concomitant of the doctrine of a church professing to have a code or rule of faith. Indeed, we have good reason to suspect that some religious groups that emphasize the importance of 'salvation' do so at least partly because they have little else to say in defence of the reasonableness of their faith. The idea of 'salvation' has often been exploited. None of these things would matter much here, of course, were it not for the fact that so much intolerance and persecution have grown out of the desire to 'save' souls. I realize that belief in salvation is *in fact* an actual if not integral part of many or even most religious creeds. We have neither a reason nor a right to expect it to disappear suddenly from these creeds. I do think it important, however, that religious leaders and 'witnesses' not be taken in by arguments like Wiseman's, for if they are, they are going to emphasize this aspect of religion at the expense of other more important aspects.

A MATTER OF SHARING

I have not clearly defined the terms 'exclusivism' and 'universalism.' These are not terms from ordinary language, and even students of philosophy and theology are apt to find them rather ambiguous. In point of fact, the terms are only slightly more obscure than the various features of religions with which they are likely to be associated. Some will regard a person as a religious 'universalist' if he holds that *all* human beings can be 'saved' even if they do not hold all the beliefs of his group. Some will see the religious universalist as the person who holds that *all* human beings should be aggressively persuaded or even forced to adopt the beliefs of his group. There are as many forms of religious 'universalism' as there are ways of using the term 'all' when talking about religions. And as I observed earlier, there are as many forms of religious exclusivism as there are ways of using the word 'only' when talking about religions. Berdyaev associates Jewish 'exclusiveness' with loyalty to one's own things and people *only*, while Wiseman's defence of the doctrine of exclusive salvation amounts to a defence of the church's right to hold that *only* its members will be saved.

Religions combine exclusivistic and universalistic elements. In prescribing certain things and proscribing others, religions are doing a good deal of excluding; and in affirming that all men will be better off if they think and act in certain ways, religions are truly universalistic. But when we reflect on the statements of Berdyaev and Wiseman, we soon realize that their talk about the 'all' and the 'only' is not merely name-calling or rationalizing. Different religious groups do blend exclusivistic and universalistic elements in different ways, and the differences in the modes of blending are reflected in obvious and important differences between, say, Judaism and Roman Catholicism, or the major western and eastern faiths. Every religious denomination eventually arrives at its own general pedagogical strategy or, better yet, at its own method of sharing its spiritual wealth with others.

When one attends a Roman Catholic religious service, one has concrete evidence of the church's 'catholicism'; one can see for oneself how the church has opened its doors for people of all races, nationalities, and ethnic backgrounds. One has proof of the church's eagerness to share its spiritual wealth with others. Indeed, the church has often been prepared to force its spiritual wealth on others, even at the risk of depriving them of whatever spiritual wealth they already have. When one attends a Jewish religious service, one may well be struck by the dearth of black and yellow and pink faces; perhaps one will be reminded of the Jews' 'soft sell,' or maybe of the tremendous pressures put on people to avoid or abandon Judaism. Yet, what student of history can deny that the Jews have shared their spiritual wealth with the gentiles? Could Christianity and Islam have developed as they have if the Jews had kept their religious ideas and values hidden from the nations? But for every strategy of sharing wealth, there is a risk to be taken, a price to be paid.

7

Religious tolerance and the state

As serious as the intolerance of isolated individuals is, it is the intolerance of men in groups that commands the lion's share of our attention. Of all the communities into which a human being enters, the state is by far the most powerful, at least in the temporal realm, and state-sanctioned religious persecution is the worst kind of all. Political 'freedom of religion' is a relatively modern ideal, and even now religious liberty is not as widespread as we often like to believe. Religious liberty should not be taken for granted anywhere at any time; it is something that people must constantly struggle to maintain. For as we saw earlier, religious pluralism has its intelligent critics as well as its irrational, fanatic ones. Unfortunately, the concept of religious liberty is an extremely nebulous one, and so we should not be surprised that what one person considers political toleration of religion another considers political repression.

THE MYTH OF ABSOLUTE RELIGIOUS LIBERTY

That religious liberty is extremely limited in theocratic and authoritarian states is something we all know. But consider a liberal society like the American, one that is well known for its commitment to political toleration of religious minorities. The First Amendment to the United States Constitution guarantees Americans that the United States Congress 'shall make no law respecting an establishment of religion, or prohibiting the free exercise thereof.' Americans are justly proud of their nation's tradition of religious toleration and religious liberty. But freedom of religion is no more an *absolute* freedom in the United States than it is anywhere else. And it is no more an *absolute* freedom than freedom of speech or freedom of the press. Just as there are laws that prohibit, say, slander and libel, there are laws that prohibit what are regarded as abuses of religious liberty. For example, in the case of *Chaplinsky* vs *New Hampshire*, the United States Supreme Court unanimously affirmed the conviction of a Jehovah's Witness who had used derisive language in responding to remarks of a city marshal. The court's opinion, written by Justice Murphy, is revealing: 'We cannot conceive that cursing a public officer is the exercise of religion in any sense of the term. But even if the activities of the appellant which preceded the incident could be viewed as religious in character, and therefore entitled to the protection of the Fourteenth Amendment, they would not cloak him with immunity from the legal consequences for concomitant acts committed in violation of a valid criminal statute.'[1]

Legislatures and courts in the United States, as in areas where religious liberty is not the norm, regularly take it upon themselves to determine what is genuinely religious and what is not. (They do so, for example, when determining what kinds of institutions should be eligible for tax exemptions or public aid.) Also, they prosecute men whose violation of a criminal statute is directly or indirectly related to their religious convictions. Chaplinsky's cursing may not have been the exercise of religion; but American courts have prosecuted people for refusing, on religious grounds, to send their children to accredited schools or to salute the flag. They have also prosecuted people for encouraging children under their care to sell religious literature and even for 'holding a religious meeting in a public park without a permit as required by ordinance, even though [they have] properly sought that permit and been arbitrarily and illegally refused by those responsible for administering the ordinance ...'[2]

The power of the state to legislate and to enforce its laws is theoretically a threat to all religious believers. No matter what the state legislates, it is *possible* that someone will object to the legislation on religious grounds. Major religious bodies may not be troubled by the state's passing of law x, but members of some obscure sect may well find law x to be highly objectionable. The decisions of the state reflect the opinions of those people in the society who have political power; this state of affairs characterizes a democratic, pluralistic society as much as a theocratic, authoritarian one. There is, on the whole, more religious liberty in our society for those who belong to large, powerful religious bodies than for those who belong to small sects (though much depends on the actual beliefs in question). Moreover, complete separation of church and state is impossible. Civil laws often, as in the case of those relating to marriage, reflect religious traditions of the largest religious groups in the society. Political leaders are not as worried about offending religious minorities as they are about offending the religious majority. At the same time, even those pluralists who defend the ideal of separation of church and state usually admit that the state has the upper hand. What kind of separation exists between two institutions when one is ultimately subject to the domination of the other? Unlike, say, the society of the Soviet Union, our society is one in which religion per se is tolerated or even encouraged. But the fact remains that in our society religious people depend, in both theory and practice, on the grace of political leaders who may or may not share their religious beliefs.

Though the First Amendment is couched in terms that suggest that religious liberty is an absolute freedom in the United States, there are clearly theoretical and practical limits to religious freedom even in American society. There is relatively more political toleration of religious minorities in the United States than there is in, say, Saudi Arabia or Spain or the Soviet Union; still, there are limits to what the American government will tolerate in the way of 'free exercise' of religion. Now, for better or for worse, the authors of the First Amendment did not specify any criteria for determining when exactly the free exercise of religion should be curtailed. They did not set down what they considered to be the proper limits of religious liberty, the proper limits to the state's toleration of religious behaviour. They left it to future generations of jurists to decide what those proper limits are. In making decisions of this kind, jurists have been guided by various philosophical presuppositions as well as by purely technical, legal considerations. Yet, only a few philosophers (for instance, Sidney Hook) have seen the subject of religious liberty as one that urgently demands close philosophical analysis, and only a few political theorists (for example, Milton Konvitz) have made a serious effort to examine the conceptual underpinning of the relevant legal and political problems.[3]

Say that we were in a position to modify the First Amendment in such a way that it would no longer leave the mistaken impression that the United States Constitution guarantees Americans *absolute* religious freedom. What kind of proviso would it be advisable for us to add to the 'free exercise' clause? Or would the First Amendment have to be completely revised? The First Amendment says that Congress *shall make no law* prohibiting the free exercise of religion, but *any* law theoretically puts limitations on the free exercise of religion. The state will tolerate only so much in the way of religious activity. The government will not put up with religious behaviour that conflicts dramatically with the state-sanctioned way of life. Every government expects and requires churches to accommodate themselves to certain basic demands of the civil law (though in a theocracy, of course, the civil law reflects the decisions of the ecclesiastical authorities of a particular, 'established' church).

People are prosecuted for murdering, stealing, cursing public officers, and so forth, whether or not they conceive of their criminal acts as somehow religious. People are also prosecuted, even in democratic societies, for doing things that are not nearly as serious as murdering or stealing: keeping their shops open on someone else's Sabbath, distributing literature for the purpose of proselytizing, buying contraceptive devices, and so on. Some criminal acts are obviously much more serious than others, and many should not even be criminal acts. Almost a hundred years ago, Justice Field, delivering the court opinion on a case involving polygamy, argued that 'however free the exercise of religion may be, it must be subordinate to the criminal laws of the country, passed with reference to actions regarded by general consent as properly the subject of punitive legislation.'[4] P.B. Kurland has made a profound observation about this particular court opinion: 'That such a thesis would have sustained outlawry of the mass, that it would have sustained most of the Tudor legislation restricting Catholics and most of the legislation that forced religious dissenters to leave the shores of Europe for haven in the New World, apparently gave concern to no member of the Court.'[5]

Can the First Amendment, or any liberal principle like it, be patched up so that it does not leave the mistaken impression that the state will tolerate *anything* done in the name of religion? Can it be patched up in such a way that it will enable a liberal government to avoid both *indiscriminate tolerance* and *intolerance*? Many political scientists and legal scholars think so, but the fact remains that the American and Canadian and British governments have always been committed to the position that they can and must make laws that *in effect* prohibit the free exercise of religion – not the exercise of Anglicanism or Methodism or Catholicism or even Judaism, but of religion in general. If they were not committed to this position, they would not make any laws at all or attempt to enforce laws. Now, the authors of the First Amendment to the u.s. Constitution had certain specific problems in mind, problems that were primarily concrete rather than theoretical or philosophical.[6]

Instead of dealing directly with these problems, they committed themselves publicly to what we have seen to be an untenable or at least impracticable principle.

When we consider the First Amendment in terms of its historical context, we see that it is an expression of goodwill, an attempt by political leaders to assure religious people in a non-theocratic, pluralistic society that the government will not interfere with the exercise of religion as much as other governments do. It is an announcement to the peoples of the world that the u.s. government is reluctant to enter into religious matters. But the expression of goodwill is an overstatement. The problem here is not simply one of interpretation, or even one of finding the appropriate proviso to tack on to the 'free exercise' clause. It is something more fundamental. By its laws, the government limits the free exercise of religion, and so in an important sense it makes laws that prohibit the free exercise of religion.

Anglicans, Methodists, Catholics, and Jews are all opposed to murder, theft, and polygamy. They do not have to be told by the civil authorities that it is wrong to murder, steal, or have more than one spouse. Civil laws against murder, theft, and polygamy do not pose a threat to their religious way of life. Still, there are also religious fanatics of various persuasions, and their religious leaders often encourage them to do things that are generally regarded as immoral. The state offers its citizens protection from such fanatics. But whatever consolation we derive from knowing that the state has the power to check religious fanaticism cannot fully compensate for the fears that many of us have about the unrestrained power of the state.

Many people in our society tend to admire the average clergyman more than the average politician. Though they may respect Supreme Court justices more than other politicians and lawyers, they often mistrust most of the men who actually *make* our laws.[7] Protestants often worry about the influence of Catholic legislators and lobbyists, and Catholics often worry about the influence of Protestant leaders; but it does not follow that Protestants and Catholics look up to secular or atheistic politicians. Most of us are happy to see the government keeping other people's religious activities 'in line'; but we are not nearly as happy when we see the government dictating policy to our own religious leaders. As Kurland has rightly observed, even democratic governments can be rather arbitrary in serving the interests of one religious group more than those of another. Here is a potential problem in democratic societies as well as undemocratic ones, for elected officials are mere mortals who, lacking the wisdom of Plato's ideal philosopher-kings, often have strange ideas about what actions are properly the subject of punitive legislation. Governments can arbitrarily restrict religious freedom even when they are not serving the religious interests of a particular 'established' church or group of churches. What makes these facts all the more disturbing is that the state usually maintains an army and a police force to enforce its laws, while the church's principal means of defence against the state's aggression is simply a moral or political one.

We have seen now that not only is there no absolute religious liberty, but *any* law theoretically represents a limiting of religious liberty. And not only is no state willing to tolerate everything done in the name of religion, but for a variety of reasons there cannot be complete separation of church and state, of the religious and the secular. Therefore, there is little value in revising a principle like the First Amendment in such a way that it promises that the government shall make no law prohibiting the free exercise of religion *except when*, etc., etc. If we revised the First Amendment along these lines, we would have to add an indefinitely long list of exceptions. It has been suggested that such exceptions all have something important in common, but whatever that something is, it is nothing very profound. If we follow Justice Field's lead, we may end up believing that a government should make no law prohibiting the free exercise of religion except when religious activities are in violation of criminal laws 'passed with reference to actions regarded by general consent as properly the subject of punitive legislation.' But what does this amount to believing? That the state should make no law prohibiting the free exercise of religion *except when it does*? That it should make no law prohibiting the free exercise of religion *except when people 'generally' feel it should*? What appears to be a healthy democratic position is really a dangerous conventionalistic one; it saves the state from indiscriminate tolerance but at the expense of encouraging intolerance. It justifies the state's curbing the activities of certain groups of religious fanatics, but it can also justify the oppression of relatively powerless and innocuous religious minorities.

When we remember that *any* law theoretically represents a limiting of religious freedom, we see that the key question is when the government has a right to pass *any* laws. A government that derives its powers from the consent of the governed aims at securing certain rights, and it carries out its aim by performing certain specific tasks, for instance, establishing justice, ensuring domestic tranquillity, promoting the general welfare. It is because we value justice and domestic tranquillity that we are prepared to tolerate a government and its laws. But it is a sad fact that many governments do not establish justice or ensure domestic tranquillity, and an equally sad one that even healthy governments have serious lapses. Often religious groups do more to promote justice and domestic tranquillity than civil governments do. Why, then, should we follow those supposedly 'liberal' thinkers who argue that in cases of conflict between the state and a church, the judgment of the state should (or must) take precedence over that of the church?

Sometimes churches simply cannot accommodate their teachings or practices to the demands of the state. That there are not more confrontations between church and state only goes to show how weak most modern churches and religious leaders are. Usually, willingness to acquiesce to immoral government policies is based on considerations of expediency rather than considerations of church doctrine. I cannot think of any religion that does not make ethical prescriptions that *may* come into conflict with the demands of civil governments. And so we cannot understand the proper limits of religious liberty – or of political toleration of religious activities – in terms of the specific kinds of laws a government has a right to pass. When the First Amendment was written, political leaders had good reason to fear the intolerance of powerful churches. But many years have passed since the First Amendment was written. Perhaps the pendulum has swung to the other side, and it is the 'secular' state's power that is to be feared more.

THE PROPER LIMITS OF POLITICAL TOLERATION

The only acceptable justification for the state's restricting religious freedom is a *moral* one. Even prudential justifications must conform to the demands of morality. Religious activities can be moral or immoral; so can civil laws. Neither church nor state has a monopoly on morality; even if one believes that certain political or ecclesiastical leaders are in possession of a perfectly true ethical *doctrine*, one can still see that these leaders make errors in moral *judgment* or *reasoning*. It is sometimes said that while the state speaks for all its citizens, a particular church (in a pluralistic society) only speaks for some of the state's citizens. But when we strongly disagree, on moral grounds, with the government's legislation, is the state really speaking 'for us'? Moral or religious people cannot regard grossly unethical laws as acceptable. Moreover, a Roman

Catholic can agree with Quakers and Lutherans and Mormons that a certain law is immoral, and so another man's church can sometimes speak 'for us' more effectively than our government.

Since we should be moral and act morally, when there is a conflict between our church and our state on a serious moral issue we should follow whichever one is promoting morality or acting in accordance with it. Indeed we should act morally even if doing so requires us to go against the demands of both church *and* state. It is, of course, often difficult to discern what the moral course to follow is in a given situation. In such situations, we often look to both church and state for guidance. But even here, blind obedience is not morally acceptable. All of these facts suggest that the proper limit to religious liberty is morality itself. When the state properly restricts religious freedom, when it refuses to tolerate immoral religious activities (for instance, those involving disturbances of the peace or the harassment of unbelievers), it is doing so as the agent of morality. However, the very same moral limits pertain to the state's proper exercise of its own legislative and executive powers. A state has no more right to promote immorality than a church does. When a government tries to force, say, the policy of racial segregation on a church, believers should give careful consideration to the value of civil disobedience.

These ideas are so simple, and their truth is so obvious, that it may be hard to believe that they are relevant to the complex problem that we have been considering. Some will argue that they are not relevant, and others will say that though they are relevant, they are too abstract to have any concrete, practical application. Some will argue that the civil government and the civil law have already taken them into consideration. Surely, however, it is important that we can appeal to an authority that is higher than both church and state, and surely, in considering the limits of action – religious, legislative, or any other kind – we would be remiss if we ignored morality and moral considerations. Still, there are different theories about the proper criterion of morality and the nature of moral judgment. Consider, for example, the famous Victorian disagreement between Gladstone and Cardinal Newman on the subject of the loyalty of English Catholics. According to Gladstone, the allegiance of English Catholics to the church is greater than their allegiance to the state, and so non-Catholic Englishmen cannot trust their Catholic compatriots when church-state conflicts arise. Newman responds by appealing to a higher authority, 'conscience.' 'Certainly,' he writes, 'if I am obliged to bring religion into after-dinner toasts, (which indeed does not seem quite the thing) I shall drink, – to the Pope, if you please, – still, to Conscience first, and to the Pope afterwards.'[8] How can one weigh his political obligation against his religious obligation unless he has taken into account his moral obligation? Even the most slavishly obedient churchgoer believes that his church's leaders have *reasons* for making the particular demands that they make.

But why associate morality with 'conscience' rather than with practical moral reasoning and practical moral wisdom? Even when understood in the way that Newman understands it, 'conscience' is a dangerous thing to appeal to, for with a moral-sense theory of moral judgment, it is hard to avoid subjectivism and relativism, and some of the worst crimes have been committed in the name of 'conscience.' We could not blame Gladstone for rejecting Newman's candidate for the highest authority. Sometimes, Gladstone seems simply to have been siding with the state rather than the church. But at other times Gladstone actually seems to have been suggesting that English Catholics tend to *substitute* 'conscience' and obedience for genuine moral judgment. But what is genuine moral judgment if not judgment based on the dictates of conscience or religious leaders?

Though there are important disagreements among philosophers about what the true criterion of morality is, most philosophers associate morality with 'acting on the basis of good reasons.' Say that our government passes a certain law that requires us to perform a certain action, *a*, which we have good reason to believe is immoral. We do not have to rely on our conscience to tell us that we should not torture, exploit, or arbitrarily slaughter our fellow human beings. There are good reasons for not doing such things; besides, chances are that our government is itself publicly committed to ideals that its immoral laws are preventing us from realizing. Similarly, if our church requires us to do *a*, we have the very same reasons for not doing it that we have when the state demands that we do it. A Catholic or Methodist or Mormon should be able to see that unreflective leaders of his church are capable of making errors in moral judgment even when they are committed in principle to the most noble ideals. In a church-state disagreement, a church can be advocating *a* while the state condemns it, or the state can be advocating *a* while the church condemns it. One is not even being rational when one justifies one's refusal to do *a*, immoral as it is, simply by saying that the state or church considers it to be improper. There is a place for respect for authority, but authoritarianism per se is not an adequate or reliable ethical theory. Therefore, it follows that one is not being completely rational when, in dealing with the rightness or wrongness of any particular action, one argues that the state's judgment must supersede the church's, or vice versa. The state's reasons and arguments may be stronger *or* weaker than the church's.

Some Roman Catholics and others may want to argue that their religious commitment requires complete obedience to the leaders of the church. If they study the writings of their most profound co-religionists, however, they will find that no tolerable church demands a blind, irrational obedience. Certainly the Catholic church does not, as Newman, a prince of his church, pointed out to Gladstone. And in pluralistic societies, ecclesiastical leaders know that they have to defend their positions on controversial ethico-political issues.

One reason why political theorists are often quick to assert that the state's judgment should supersede the church's is that they consider political leaders to be more rational than religious leaders. Supreme Court justices and even legislators do give reasons and arguments in support of their positions. Over the centuries, many religious leaders have tended to emphasize that such-and-such an action has been enjoined by a certain sacred work or revered teacher. In many societies, such as the theocratic societies of the Middle Ages, religious leaders did not have to bother providing rational defences of their demands. But in non-theocratic dictatorships, *political* leaders have not had to bother either. The fact is that neither religion nor law is identical with morality, though both religion and law are supposed to embody morality. Religious teachings and civil laws give us prescriptions for action that are ostensibly ethical rather than unethical. If religion is not identical with morality, neither is it identical with immorality or irrationality. Some churches have been known to take the arguments of moral philosophers very seriously.

The Thomism of the Roman Catholic church, for example, does not seem to me to be conspicuously inferior as a moral theory to the rough utilitarianism that underlies much North American and British law. Are we really all that surprised when we find Quaker, Catholic, Jewish, or Unitarian moralists making more sensible statements than politicians? Are we really shocked when we find religious leaders being rational in discussions of moral issues? Most of us are not. Moreover, the civil law does not necessarily reflect a philosophico-religious *consensus*. When the Catholic church disagrees with the government on a particular issue, Jews may think more of the Catholic church's argument than they do of the Supreme Court's or the legislature's.

Church-state conflicts should be resolved by reference to moral arguments. Sometimes the church or the state sees itself as transcending rationality. When it does, church-state conflicts can only be resolved by force. Reason and force are historical alternatives. If we want to avoid force, we have to make a serious effort to be rational and an equally serious effort to encourage rationality in others. And since freedom and force are at odds, rationality is a basic condition of freedom. A church that appeals *exclusively* to 'divine inspiration' is, in the eyes of the outsider, not necessarily morally superior to a state whose leaders 'think with their blood.' The methods of the Inquisition and the Gestapo are equally repulsive. Still, we all know that moral reasoning is very complex, and rational people can have serious disagreements on moral issues. Leaders of church and state can be rational and *still* disagree. So when we have seen that the proper limits of religious liberty and political toleration are *moral*, we have only discovered the general way to go about determining who is right in a particular disagreement between the state and a certain religious community within the state.

Now, the ethical relativist who believes that objective moral knowledge is impossible and that moral commitments are rather arbitrary, subjective things is going to find my talk about the 'moral limits' of liberty and toleration to be terribly naïve and empty. But those of us who take the idea of *civilization* seriously, and those of us who believe that moral reasoning is not merely sophistical eristic, have to believe that talk about morality is meaningful. The man who dismisses as empty the statement that 'state and churches should be guided by moral considerations' will end up sharing the fate of the ancient Sophists. The earliest Sophists saw their relativist teaching as an impetus to social reform; but their slickest disciples ended by espousing the view that might makes right. Those who have lost all faith in reason must accept the inevitability of raw force.

THE BALANCING OF INTERESTS

Most political restrictions of religious liberty do not involve a dramatic conflict of basic moral principles. Most are viewed primarily as matters of *prudence*, matters involving a 'balancing of interests.' Refusal to salute a flag or take an oath is not reprehensible in the way that participation in human sacrifice is. When the state forces people to do something on their Sabbath or prevents them from doing certain things on someone else's Sabbath, the state is not being guided by lofty moral principles. Indeed the state can be apologetic about certain of its restrictions of religious liberty. Instead of defending such restrictions by appealing to fundamental moral principles, it argues that while it would prefer not to make these restrictions, it is forced to do so because of prudential or practical considerations (for instance, 'It will simply cost too much for us to extend to you people these special privileges.' 'If we make an exception for your denomination, other groups will demand that we make similar exceptions for them.' 'Surely you cannot expect us to go to all that trouble so that you people can practise this ritual.').

In an opinion involving an important 1961 U.S. Supreme Court case, Justice Felix Frankfurter argued that 'if the value to society of achieving the object of a particular regulation is demonstrably outweighted by the impediment to which the regulation subjects those whose religious practices are curtailed by it, or if the object sought by the regulation could with equal effect be achieved by alternative means which do not substantially impede those religious practices, the regulation cannot be sustained.'[9] Frankfurter has told us that the state should make every reasonable effort to be tolerant of religious practices, but he has also reminded us that there are practical limits to what the state must tolerate. The state must put up with religious practices only when the 'value to society' in restricting them is 'demonstrably outweighted' by the impediment to which such a restriction would subject the religious group in question. Value? Weighing? Here we are faced with utilitarian considerations. Frankfurter has told us that the state must make some important *calculations*. Unfortunately, he has not explained to us in any detail how the state should go about doing this calculating, this weighing, this balancing.

In utilitarianism, the distinction between moral judgments and prudential judgments, when it exists at all, is blurry.[10] In a state like ours, whose ethico-legal system rests largely on utilitarian principles, there is a tendency on the part of legislators and jurists to see it as *moral* to restrict religious freedom when doing so substantially favours the interests of the overwhelming majority of the state's citizens; similarly, our leaders generally tend to see members of religious groups as *immoral* when they refuse to alter their religious practices in such a way as to make those practices conform with what is generally perceived in the society as being the way of life that promotes the greatest total happiness for the greatest number of citizens. Why, then, should a government like ours ever be apologetic about those of its restrictions that are imposed in the name of 'prudence'? One reason is that intelligent leaders recognize that determining the proper balance of interests in a given situation is often an extremely difficult task. (Notice that Frankfurter has carefully used such terms as 'demonstrably' and 'substantially.') Also, while our political and judicial leaders usually work with a utilitarian ethical theory, their justifications of certain restrictions of religious liberty suggest that they do distinguish, at some level of consciousness, between a morality of prudence or utility and a higher morality of principle or duty or justice. Many of them can see that in certain situations some people may have to pay an unfair price for helping to promote the general happiness. There are many situations in which the prudent or expedient course is an unjust one.

Religious leaders tend to have less confidence in utilitarian morality than politicians and jurists do. Not only is one's pastor apt to disagree with statesmen that a certain restriction of the pastor's religious liberty is morally justifiable, but he may well argue that the criterion to which the government officials are appealing is not a distinctively *moral* one. Many non-utilitarian liberals will support him here, although few will support him if the basis of his criticism is the presupposition that the only genuine morality is that which is grounded in religious faith.

We saw at the outset of our inquiry that there is no simple formula for determining how much a decent person or a decent society can be reasonably expected to tolerate. At one time, members of small religious minorities would have been happy if they were allowed to do just x; later they came to take their right to do x for granted, and petitioned for the right to do y; and so on. At one time, a man did not sound so callous if he asked his Mormon or Jewish or Catholic friend, 'What more do you people want? We do not kill you or make you join our church, do we?' And as I observed in the first chapter, the most we can do in this sphere is try to convince our political and judicial leaders that prudence itself dictates that we be gentle and patient with religious minorities.

We live in a society in which final decisions in cases of church-state conflict are made by the state, and so in theory religious leaders (of powerful churches as well as weak ones) must answer to political leaders. Church and state both prefer to hide this fact; to admit to it openly would be to detract from their apparent integrity. In any case, the major churches are treated reasonably well. Political officials are sensitive to the political power that large churches derive from their influence on men and women who vote in elections and in other ways pose a threat to the present regime and the present government. Many political leaders are themselves religious believers or are justly proud of our nation's impressive tradition of religious toleration. However, people who belong to the less influential churches and religious people who are not affiliated with any church do not usually fare as well in their dealings with the government as do members of large, powerful churches. Though liberty ought to be rooted in moral strength, it is more often a function of political, economic, or numerical strength.

Since absolute religious liberty is not possible in either a theocracy or a social system like ours, and since it is hard to conceive of a third, radically different approach to church-state relations, our choice – assuming that we have one – is essentially between theocracy and a system like our own. Our system is far from perfect, and there have been liberal theocracies. But history suggests that religious liberty flourishes more easily under a system of relative church-state separation than it does under a theocratic system. In our system, ultimate power rests with the state rather than the church; but the concrete, practical factors that have given rise to this state of affairs have also resulted in the state's being rather cautious in exercising its power in this area. Also, while the state places restrictions on religious liberty, it acts as well to protect religious liberty and to aid churches in other ways. So the churches do get something in return for their willingness to acquiesce to the limited demands of legislators, bureaucrats, and judges.

Nevertheless, it is important to build into our system certain mechanisms that will guarantee that the political demands will not become unreasonable. Church and state must be vigilant in promoting morality. They must control themselves, and they must use whatever power they have to check the unrestrained power of other elements in society. The most important condition of church-state harmony is church-state dialogue; and the most important condition of the latter is a shared respect for rationality and a shared commitment to the trans-cultural moral ideals.

Let us descend for the moment from the abstract to the concrete. Legislators and jurists in our society like to believe that religious people (and other people too) have an adequate voice in political decision-making. People can vote, run for office, lobby, write pamphlets and letters to newspaper editors, criticize politicians from the pulpit and banquet table, and so forth. But consider these points. First, it often happens that government policy conflicts with the aims and desires of the general public, the overwhelming majority; and, at times, those who are responsible for formulating government policy consciously fly in the face of popular sentiment. Sometimes decent people have reason to be thankful for the independence of enlightened political leaders. Still, we can see that the influence of our input is not always all that great, that even in a democracy it is possible for political leaders to act without the consent of the governed.

Secondly, whose voice is paid the most attention? Is it the most moral man's or the most rational man's? Is it the moral philosopher's or the theologian's? Rarely. As a general rule, one receives attention in proportion to one's political influence. Courts do, as a matter of course, consult 'authorities'; so do legislative committees and executive agencies. But how does one come to be regarded as an authority, and how much influence does the genuine authority's judgment have? It is worth while considering the kind of men who are elected to high political office or even appointed to the highest courts in the land. How often are they our finest moral teachers? Is the state run by those who have wisdom in their soul or by those who can convince the voters that they are 'the people's friends'? To make matters worse, we have acquiesced to the increasing domination of our political life by members of the legal profession. How ironic, for many people have little confidence in the moral powers of lawyers, even those lawyers who are now judges. Whether or not Plato is right in arguing that lawyers are by their very nature untrustworthy, it is clear that we pay a high price for allowing lawyers to dominate the affairs of the state. Lawyers and judges speak in their own technical language and it is hard for them to engage in meaningful dialogue with those who do not speak their language or share their presuppositions. As a result, the ideas religious leaders and other 'authorities' present to the courts, legislative committees, and executive agencies end up being put in a legal sieve, and often all that is saved are the minutiae rather than the wisdom.

The appropriate remedy is obvious enough. In cases of church-state conflict, final decisions should be made by those who are capable of making an intelligent, rational, moral decision based on knowledge of the background, circumstances, and implications of the particular case. Who are these people? Judges and jurors? Certainly these men *can* be rational, moral, and knowledgeable; but do they have sufficient expertise? Would it not be safer to have them *share* their decision-making power with theologians, representatives of the churches, and students of comparative religion? Must religious leaders be limited to playing only an *advisory* role? Does not a liberal principle like the First Amendment *demand* that churchmen be allowed to play a much greater role than they now do in making judgments about matters that affect them.

Consider possible objections. 'Students of religion do not have sufficient knowledge of legal matters to be able to participate in legal decision-making on an equal basis with legal scholars.' People who raise such an objection should consider the corresponding limits to the jurist's religious, theological, and philosophical knowledge. Besides, there is nothing that prevents students of religion from acquiring legal knowledge. 'There is so much disagreement among religious leaders that they can hardly be expected to reach a consensus.' Almost all religious leaders, however, look to the same set of basic, trans-cultural moral absolutes. There is no evidence that their disagreements are more profound than disagreements among politicians and jurists, who are often conspicuously left-wing or right-wing. 'The government should not formally "recognize" religion.' But why not? It will not go away any sooner. On the contrary, it is one of the most important of all cultural phenomena. The law cannot ignore it; the First Amendment does not ignore it; no student of the human condition should ignore it. 'Religion should not be seen as being above the law.' Nor should it be seen as being below the law. Erastianism is not obviously superior or preferable to theocracy. If we are to take the idea of relative church-state separation seriously, are we not forced to give churchmen a meaningful role in dealing with church-state conflicts? 'If the government caters to the interests of religious groups, it should also cater to the interests of other groups. Why give religious groups preferential treatment?' The government, of course, should concern itself with the interests of all of the state's residents. But the church is very different from other institutions. It is not simply a club or a party; its members associate it with the meaning of life, human destiny, the world to come, the word of God. It is accepted by its members as a great moral teacher and guide. Still, I am not sure that other groups should *not* be allowed to have a stronger voice in political and judicial decision-making. I only contend that for historical and philosophical reasons, reflected in principles like the First Amendment, a church merits special and immediate consideration.

'We do not really need such a reform. The legislatures and courts are doing a fairly good job.' Some would disagree with this assessment. I shall not. But what does the future hold? Who will sit on the highest courts in the land fifty or a hundred years from now? 'Practical considerations suggest that such a reform is impossible. Introducing this kind of mechanism would spoil the whole criminal justice system.' I would like to see this objection spelled out. *Why* would such a mechanism ruin our whole legal system? 'This policy is a reactionary policy; it brings us back a step closer to theocracy.' People who argue in this way not only have too much confidence in the liberalism of political leaders, but also do not understand what a theocracy is.

But there is little point in my speaking further about this 'remedy.' I am not sure how we could go about implementing such a policy, and in any event, secular leaders are not likely to be excited by the prospect of having to share their decision-making power with religious leaders, and all the churches combined do not have the influence to force the government to share its power. People in our society, for understandable reasons, feel relatively comfortable with the status quo, and while they are sensitive to political corruption and incompetence, they also know that power corrupts religious leaders too.

AN IMPORTANT PRINCIPLE OF POLITICAL PHILOSOPHY

Some of you may believe that the subjects that we have been considering have little to do with the topic of religious tolerance. They have to do with politics and law. But we cannot understand religious tolerance if we do not have any understanding of political toleration of religious activities. In fact, some people associate 'religious toleration' *exclusively* with what governments are willing to put up with in the way of unconventional religious behaviour. For example, Henry Kamen, who has written on the history of religious toleration, tells us that 'in its broadest sense, toleration can be understood to mean the concession of liberty to those who dissent in religion.' Yet, his examples of religious toleration and intolerance are all political ones.[11]

In my comments on religious tolerance and the state, I have avoided speaking about concrete political and legal problems. I have tried to show that there are theoretical as well as practical obstacles to absolute religious freedom and absolute separation of church and state; and I have spoken a bit about the moral limits of political toleration of religion. If I have not said more about the political dimension of religious tolerating, it is not only because I am aware that much has been said and written about this dimension of toleration, but also because I believe that in the last analysis the democratic state is tolerant in proportion to the tolerance of the individual citizens who make it up. In a dictatorship, an enlightened despot can overrule the demands of the intolerant rabble, or a wicked tyrant can ignore the public demand for political toleration of religious activities. In a society like ours, liberal political leaders can try to encourage the spirit of religious tolerance, and to some extent they can succeed in doing so. Unfortunately, most of us have gotten into the habit of expecting too much of our government and too little of our neighbours, our relatives, ourselves – the people who make up the state. And so if I have said relatively little about the political dimension of religious toleration, it is mainly because I agree with all those political philosophers who have made this important point: the proper way to go about reforming a free society is to work hard at reforming the individuals who make it up, including oneself. Direct political action is useful as a response to intolerable abuses, but the improvements it brings about, while important, are relatively short-lived.

8

The intolerant personality

Many people believe that the problem of religious intolerance is essentially a psychological one. This view is rather plausible. Intolerance is a human phenomenon; it is human beings that we speak of as being tolerant or intolerant. We see the intolerant man as having a defect in his personality: a flaw, an inadequacy, a vice, an incapacity, a sickness. We think that there is something wrong with him, that for one reason or other he is not the way a person ought to be. We see him as being abnormal, sick. And we look to the psychologist and the psychiatrist to explain to us why it is that the intolerant man cannot or will not accept things a man ought to accept.

I have been trying to show that the problem of religious intolerance is multi-faceted, not simply psychological. It has a *conceptual* dimension: one reason intolerance is so widespread is that many people do not understand what tolerance is or what it demands; many intolerant people actually think that they are tolerant, and liberal people usually have trouble explaining to them why they are wrong. It has an *epistemological* dimension: religious intolerance generally involves prejudice, bad judgment, insufficient evidence, misinterpretation of data, unsound reasoning. It has a *theological* dimension: intolerant men often see their religious commitments as requiring them to wage a war against all forms of 'idolatry' and 'unbelief,' and to make converts by any and every means available, no matter how unwholesome it may seem; and indeed some of the most important religious teachers and leaders have laid the groundwork for popular intolerance. The problem even has an important *utilitarian* dimension: many men are convinced that the consequences of tolerating men of other faiths will be disastrous, that it is better to be branded as 'intolerant' than to stand by idly as one's society is destroyed by 'secularism' or by foolish acquiescence to the unreasonable demands of exotic religious sects.

And so if we are to minimize the amount of religious intolerance in the world, we must do more than disseminate the reports of psychologists and psychiatrists. We must teach those around us what it *means* to be tolerant. We must show people how to reason properly, how to be logical, how to make reasonable judgments. We must attack lies and slanders and distorted perceptions. We must find ways of inducing religious leaders to play down those aspects of their church's doctrine that are maleficent or obstacles to civilization. We must construct utilitarian and other ethical arguments for use against those who defend religious persecution in the name of 'prudence.' Above all, we must help others to appreciate – and constantly remind ourselves of – the importance of civilization.

Yet, I myself have already admitted that the *concept* of tolerance is essentially a psychological one. In contrasting the concepts of intolerance and prejudice, I remarked that while the latter is primarily epistemological, the former is primarily psychological. Judgments are true or false; acceptances are not. We speak of certain people as good judges; we never speak of people as good 'accepters.' We can see that accepting is a rather more subjective matter than judging. Now, when I say that the concept of intolerance is a psychological concept rather than an epistemological one, I am not saying that only psychologists and psychiatrists can understand and cure religious intolerance; nor am I saying that the *problem* of intolerance is a one-dimensional, psychological problem. I am saying that religious intolerance involves more than simply being in error; it involves the state of the *psyche*. If tolerance is a virtue, then intolerance is a vice. Virtues and vices are the determinants of the relative health of the psyche, the soul, the personality. And we cannot deny that the problem of religious intolerance has, among others, a psychological dimension. So let us consider now some philosophical theories of how the vice of religious intolerance develops in the soul.

SUPERSTITION AND ENTHUSIASM

In an interesting 1741 essay, 'Of Superstition and Enthusiasm,' the Scottish philosopher David Hume discusses 'the corruptions of religion.' In Hume's view, 'false religion' should not be identified with heterodoxy but with ignorance and irrationality. A man well ahead of his time,

Hume argued that religious people worry too much about minor disagreements on doctrinal matters and too little about persecutions, religious wars, bigotry, and obstacles to civil liberty. In his essay, however, he also draws our attention to what he considers to be a significant difference between the 'superstition' of Catholic and Anglican bigots and the 'enthusiasm' of sectarian bigots (for instance, Quakers, Presbyterians, Anabaptists). He suggests that superstition and enthusiasm are two basic forms of religious corruption with different psychological origins and different social effects. Hume's psychological thesis is that superstition is rooted in *weakness and fear*, while enthusiasm is rooted in *pride and presumption*. His political thesis is that while enthusiasm leads to the most cruel disorders, it is ultimately far more innocuous than superstition.

Hume believes that his use of the terms 'superstition' and 'enthusiasm' conforms with the use of these terms in everyday language; but the names he gives to the two 'corruptions' are of secondary importance, for his main aim here is to make certain observations about the personalities of different kinds of bigots. Illness and melancholy induce many men to dread unknown, imaginary evils from unknown, imaginary agents. Hume gives the name 'superstition' to fear of these imaginary agents and the unaccountable methods taken up to appease them (ceremonies, mortifications, sacrifices, and so forth). But ignorance can also be combined with boldness and confidence. Health, strength, and prosperity often lead men to believe that they are distinguished favourites of the divine being. Hume gives the name 'enthusiasm' to this confidence in one's closeness to God and to the irrational behaviour that such confidence inspires.

Whether or not we approve of Hume's labels, we must follow him in recognizing fear and inspiration as independent sources of religious fanaticism. But Hume wants us to do more than simply take note of the two sources; he invites us to consider some of his reflections on the importance of his distinction. First, superstition is favourable to priestly power, while enthusiasm is contrary to it. The weak, fearful man considers himself unworthy of approaching God, so he turns to priests to approach God *for* him. These friends and servants end up as authorities, tyrants of the people. Enthusiasts, in contrast, have no use for priests since they consider themselves specially favoured by God. Secondly, though enthusiasts, being bold, are furious and dramatic at first, they sink into coolness in religious matters, for they do not acknowledge any authority whose interest it is to support the religious spirit. But superstition gradually renders men tame and submissive to priestly authorities who eventually come to be tyrants and disturbers of human society, persecutors who throw society into dismal convulsions in order to maintain or increase their influence. Thirdly, superstition is an enemy to civil liberty, but enthusiasm is a friend to it, for while superstition makes men submissive and obedient, enthusiasm leads them to speak out and become friends to toleration and freedom of speech and worship. Hume's three speculations are all concerned with the matter of authority. The man who fears God is ultimately more dangerous to civilization than the man who regards himself as inspired, for unlike the latter, he will permanently give up his right to think and act for himself.[1]

There are many weaknesses in Hume's views about the social effects of the different forms of fanaticism. One is that it is wrong to associate authoritarianism with 'superstition' *rather than* 'enthusiasm.' Consider just one counter-example, that of the Calvinists. We all know of Calvin's contempt for priests and popery, and churches founded on Calvin's teachings tend now to be relatively democratic in structure and organization. Yet, by Hume's criterion, Calvin would seem to have been more 'superstitious' than 'enthusiastic.' Calvin argues in the *Institutes* that human beings are vitiated and depraved, convicted and condemned in the sight of God. If anyone should be afraid to approach God directly, it is the Calvinist. Calvin's Geneva was a society in which submission and obedience are obligatory; somehow Calvinist principles also gave rise to democratic church government. In any case, Hume's conception of the authority of priests is exaggerated. The intelligent layman in the Catholic or Anglican church knows that he is eligible to study for the priesthood, but he elects instead to study for a career in business or law or the theatre, and accordingly he freely acquiesces to the judgment of priests in religious matters. The priesthood is not hereditary, and one becomes a priest by being educated and becoming less ignorant than the masses, the very masses that Hume would surely admit are not fit to govern.

A second weakness in Hume's position is that 'enthusiasts' do not inevitably 'sink into coolness' in religious matters. Whatever 'coolness' characterizes modern Quakers or Presbyterians seems to be absent among such other 'enthusiasts' as Mormons, Jehovah's Witnesses, and fire-breathing Baptist evangelists from the American 'Bible Belt.' Compared to most fundamentalist 'enthusiasts,' the Anglican or Roman Catholic is relatively 'cool.' And again, it is by no means obvious that priests are tyrants who oppose civil liberty and throw society into 'dismal convulsions' in order to preserve their influence. No one can deny that Catholic and also Anglican priests have been responsible for all sorts of evils: persecutions, religious wars, social unrest, economic injustice, and so forth. But Hume has not established that priests are *necessarily* tyrants, as he thinks he has. Power tends to corrupt, whether it is in the hands of religious or secular leaders. Perhaps if Hume were alive today, he would be happier to see power in the hands of priests than in the hands of political hacks, journalists, radio personalities, or businessmen. In his generation, liberals and social reformers looked to the state to correct errors that were largely the responsibility of the churches, but in our society, materialistic tyrants are much more of a threat than religious leaders, who have come to be counted, in increasing numbers, among the liberals.

What interests us most, however, is Hume's *psychology* of religious 'corruption.' Hume, we must remember, had an axe to grind; though he looked unfavourably on all ecclesiastical religion, he was primarily anti-Catholic (and opposed to Catholic influences in Anglicanism). In the essay that we have been considering, Hume is saying to his co-religionists that they should not let their worries about Protestant sectarians blind them to the fact that their real enemies are popery and High-Church Anglicanism. Still, whatever we think of his motives, we have to recognize that Hume has made an important point about religious fanaticism and intolerance: religious 'corruptions' do not all have the same psychological origin. In fact, Hume has carried this point a step further and argued that fanaticism may result from diametrically opposed psychological attitudes, undue humility and excessive self-confidence, fear and pride, weakness and strength. Even many modern students of psychology of religion still believe that there is a single 'intolerant personality,' and that as soon as we come to understand it, we shall have the solution to the whole problem of religious intolerance. Hume was actually ahead of his time in seeing the 'authoritarian personality' as being at the core of much religious fanaticism and intolerance. But he also went to great pains to point out that not *all* intolerance is the result of an obsessive respect for authority.

Hume, however, did not carry this point as far as he should have. His psychology of religious 'corruption' rests on a distinction between two basic species of fanaticism. But why are there only two? Following an earlier religious liberal, Spinoza, Hume argues that all serious religious corruption stems from ignorance rather than heterodoxy. He then adds two formulae: superstition = ignorance + weakness (fear, undue humility); and enthusiasm = ignorance + boldness (confidence, pride). Undue humility and excessive confidence are respectively vices of deficiency and of excess; the virtue that corresponds to them is a sort of bravery or self-respect.[2] But the combination of any vice with ignorance is capable of having a corrupting influence on religion. Certainly undue humility and excessive confidence or pride are not the only vices, or even the most important vices. The combination of ignorance and *profligacy* or of ignorance and *avarice* is apt to produce serious corruptions of true religion. Why, then, does Hume put so much emphasis on one pair of vices? The answer is that Hume is trying to explain the *fact* of religious corruption; he is starting with the assumption that Catholicism and Protestant sectarianism are clear-cut, paradigm cases of false religion, and he is pointing to the vices of 'weakness' and 'boldness' because they serve to explain why Catholicism and Protestant sectarianism are (different kinds of) religious corruptions. But a Catholic, Quaker, or Presbyterian can argue that Hume and his co-religionists have combined ignorance with some other and more important vice (for instance, greed). So Hume's isolating of 'weakness' and 'boldness' as the most important corrupting influences on religion represents a very narrow and selective bit of empirical psychology.

And there is another weakness in Hume's psychology of religious 'corruption.' 'Superstition' and 'enthusiasm' (and 'weakness' and 'boldness') can go hand in hand; they are not simply species. The Roman Catholic, though weak and fearful in one sense, is confident that God is with him; the Quaker or Anabaptist, though bold in one sense, also has a genuine fear of God. So it is misleading to say that some are weak while others are bold. Human personality cannot be analysed in terms of a handful of one-word categories. Hume has directed our attention to two important sources of religious fanaticism – fear of imaginary evils and confidence in one's closeness to God – but his explanation of these phenomena is sketchy, and he has neglected equally important sources, both non-psychological (which we have already considered) and psychological (which we will be considering shortly).

I have a friend, a reformed alcoholic, who would, when inebriated, become violently intolerant. When he sobered up, he would apologize to me for his remarks and lament, 'People from my cultural background are brought up to believe and say these things; I really don't understand them, and I don't mean anyone any harm.' I see no evidence that this man, an Anglican, ever had a fear of imaginary evils or a confidence in his closeness to God. When he drank, however, he was a dangerously intolerant person. The vice of drunkenness was definitely a basic contributory factor to his religious intolerance. When drunk, he would repeat outrageous slogans he himself did not understand; when sober, he is a remarkably tolerant and liberal person. Cases like his remind us that the origin of religious intolerance cannot always be explained by words like 'pride' and 'fear' and 'authoritarianism.' But it can fairly be asked how the slogans my friend repeated first originated. They could not have arisen solely as a result of drunkenness. What about the human psyche predisposes us to religious intolerance? Why do even the most liberal of us have to struggle to remain consistently tolerant?

INTOLERANCE AS IMMORALITY

The intolerant man is one who does not put up with something that he ought to put up with. Intolerance involves unwarranted refusal, unwarranted rejection. This refusal, this rejection, may or may not be an act of the will. A man may not accept things because he *cannot* accept them, because he is *unable* to accept them, because he is 'driven' to reject them. When a man is somehow compelled to reject things that he ought to accept, his intolerance is a disease, like alcoholism or drug addiction. When intolerance has this pathological character, when a man is wholly 'determined' to reject the things that he rejects, there is little use in trying to persuade him to put up with these things. Like the alcoholic or the drug addict, this man needs medical care. The behaviourist psychologist, believing as he does that everything is 'determined' and that 'free will' is a myth, has to see all intolerance as a kind of disease. But the rest of us, believing as we do that men are generally free and responsible moral agents, distinguish between the sickness of the body and the *immorality* of the 'soul' or personality. Most of us can sympathize with the genuine alcoholic; but we also believe that some men who drink too much are not addicted but simply immoral. We tell them that they lack will-power and that they can stop drinking if they really want to. All of the major religions of the world teach that a human being is, by and large and for all practical purposes, a free agent who is morally responsible for his actions. Christians and Moslems and Jews and Buddhists all believe that as a general rule a man *can* and *should* accept those things that he ought to accept. If we did not believe in free will, we would not even say that a man *ought* to accept certain things; by using the normative term 'ought' we show that we are committed to the belief that men have some control over their behaviour.

Now, I am not a behaviourist psychologist or psychiatrist, and I have nothing very profound to say about intolerance as a disease; and I am grateful for the fact that there are people who study and deal with this sickness. However, I do have some things to say about that intolerance which represents a kind of immorality, that intolerance which men have the power to curb.

According to what I shall call the 'classical' theory of human behaviour, a human being acts on the basis of his aims, desires, or wants. If men had no aims, no desires, they would not do anything, they would not be agents. But men, of course, do have aims or desires, and they regard some of these aims and desires as more important than others. They place a certain *value* on each of their aims or desires, and for that reason we speak of their aims or desires as 'values.' We also believe that men generally know what they value, what they want, and in what order of importance, and that the ordering of one's values is largely a matter of personal choice, personal commitment. The highest of our aims are often called 'aspirations' or 'ideals.' The lowest and most physical, those that we have the least control over, are often called 'appetites' or 'drives.'

Here are some different kinds of things that men have been known to value: survival, self-preservation; avoidance of pain; pleasure; appreciation of beautiful objects; companionship; being loved; being famous; being wealthy; playing chess; smoking fine cigars; dancing; peace of mind; wisdom; social reform; salvation. No one believes that playing chess is more important than avoiding pain or that smoking fine cigars is more important than being loved. We do not actually assign an exact number of 'points' to each of our aims; but we have a rough, workable idea of how much we value different things.

Some aspirations are trans-cultural and universal among those people that we consider civilized; these are, as we have seen, the desires for peace, prosperity, wisdom, love, self-realization, social justice, and so forth. Some men are so obsessed with one or more of these ideals that they concentrate almost all of their attention on this ideal or group of ideals and suppress all of their other desires. Most men, however, while valuing certain things much more than others, seek variety and a wide range of experiences, and so they pursue many different and unrelated aims (for instance, they want to play chess in the morning and fight for social reform in the afternoon). According to many modern psychologists, human behaviour is basically determined by latent drives, appetites of which human beings are ordinarily not conscious or aware. Anyone who knows what is involved in making a rational decision between two alternative courses of action also knows that this kind of deterministic theory of human behaviour is, from a pragmatic if not philosophical point of view, rather naïve; for no matter what the psychoanalyst or behaviourist says, we still have to go on with the business of weighing alternatives, making decisions, and living a life. Or as certain existentialists say, we are condemned to freedom.

I solicit your indulgence now as I engage in a bit of metaphysical theorizing. Some version of what I shall now be saying has been affirmed or at least suggested by many great religious teachers and by certain modern humanistic psychologists. But I shall not pretend to be stating any facts here; my aim right now is merely to offer a simple philosophical model for interpreting certain data.

Though the universe is essentially good, it contains a concrete element of evil; similarly, though a human being is essentially good (having been created, perhaps, in the image of God), there is an evil dimension to his personality. Though people are basically creative, productive beings who seek to promote civilization, they also have a negative, destructive streak in their personality; corresponding to every positive aim or value that they have, there is also a negative, destructive urge. Even the basic desire to survive is complemented by a self-destructive tendency. The negative dimension of human personality can never be wholly annihilated but only suppressed to a certain degree. Similarly, the negative dimension of human society, 'barbarism,' can never be wholly annihilated but only kept in check by the forces of civilization. Many people believe that good will eventually triumph over evil, but even they recognize that it is up to God – not men – to annihilate evil once and for all. In the meantime, mortals must constantly struggle to suppress this barbarous, nihilistic, destructive aspect of their society and of their own personality. In carrying on this crusade, we are often comforted by an optimistic eschatology; people who have no such eschatology (for instance, the Manicheans, fascists, atheistic existentialists, or Marxists) are especially vulnerable to sinking into barbarism.

Religious people have a special name for the negative aspect of human personality; they speak of it as the 'demonic.' Here are some of the most important demonic values: destruction, self-destruction, pain, suffering, dwelling on the morbid, violence for its own sake, suppressing rationality, being hated. Most people are, by and large, aware of the demonic elements in their personality. Most men can control the demonic side of their soul. But some cannot, and they end up as the agents of barbarism. Notice again that for every ideal of civilization, for every trans-cultural value or moral absolute, there is a corresponding demonic aim.

I realize that this talk about the demonic, the concrete presence of evil, and the reality of negative values has a speculative ring to it, perhaps even a mystical one. And it is simplistic. I make these points in my defence. First, in order to do justice to the subject of good and evil, I would have to outline and defend a complete moral philosophy, an ethical system; but as you can see, the subject of religious tolerance has already shown itself to be a big enough one to handle at this time. Secondly, I am an amateur at the art of structuralist analysis, at uncovering the hidden structures and laws that lie below surface behaviour. If I am critical of practitioners of such analysis, it is only because their zealousness often leads them to overvalue it and prevents them from paying the rational its due. It lies beyond the scope of my philosophical ability to make adequate and appropriate use of the insights of such writers as Kierkegaard, Marx, Freud, Jung, Sartre, and Lévi-Strauss. I leave it to their students to explain those things I cannot. Thirdly, I am convinced that I shall never be able to understand the worst manifestations of evil. When presented with evidence of atrocities, I am not only horrified but mystified. And I suspect that even the best practitioners of structuralist analysis are left speechless when confronted with the kind of violence that is described as 'inhuman.' Finally, one need not read too much into my talk about the demonic in order to understand what I am trying to get at – that intolerance usually involves any one of a number of forms of 'immorality' that we encounter in many different manifestations in everyday life.

What is involved in being immoral or in being immorally intolerant? There is no simple answer. We cannot simply say that the demonic or destructive elements in his personality make the immoral man immoral. Immorality takes different forms; we say that a man has acted immorally when he has done any of a number of things. 1 / A man acts immorally when he knows what is right, when he understands the importance of the highest moral ideals, but he is too weak-willed to *do* what he knows is right. If his desire to do evil is stronger than his desire to do good, then even though he knows what he should be doing, and even though at one level of consciousness he wants to do good, he is a barbarian. He is the slave of the demonic side of his personality. We have often witnessed the spectacle of religious believers committing the worst atrocities. The Grand Inquisitor, who teaches that we must love our neighbours while he tortures unbelievers, is not merely a hypocrite but a barbarian. However, some men who know what is right but are too weak-willed to *do* what is right are not barbarians. They are not barbarians because they are not succumbing to the demonic; they do not desire to do evil per se but are simply the slaves of relatively trivial desires. The man who values his pleasure or wealth over the safety of his friends and family is not a barbarian. He is a weakling; he cannot control his lower desires. But he is not pursuing evil for evil's sake; he regrets that other men are suffering, and he may even hate himself for his unwillingness to sacrifice for them. He does not hate; but he does not love enough.

2 / A man who has chosen to pursue demonic 'ideals' instead of the ideals of civilization is a barbarian and an immoralist. (We have met this man before; he is the man that the ethical relativists refuse to criticize.) This man may be *sick*, but we may be able to persuade him that the ideals of civilization are intrinsically superior to those of barbarism. One can point out to a Heliogabulus or a Hitler, for example, that he is inconsistent in doing things to other men that he does not want other men to do to him. Of course, if he thinks with his blood, and if he is not capable of being reasoned with, we have to call in the psychotherapist or lock the man up and throw away the key.

3 / A man acts immorally when he is so preoccupied with minor values that he completely forgets about relevant higher ones. The man who drinks too much or is obsessed with the pursuit of pleasure loses sight of more important things. He does not even realize that he is acting immorally, and later on, when we point out to him what he has done, he is genuinely remorseful. (If he is not remorseful, then he was not forgetful, just weak-willed or barbarous.)

4 / A man acts immorally when his emotions (for instance, anger, pity) prevent him from rationally determining the proper means of realizing relevant ideals; like the forgetful man, he does not fully realize that he is acting immorally.

5 / A man acts immorally when, as a result of having failed to consider all of the important circumstances of a situation (which he can normally have been expected to consider), he does something that has bad consequences rather than the good consequences that he had expected it

to have. (He will later tell us, 'I thought that my actions would *promote* social justice; I had no idea that my actions would result in ...') If a man cannot have been expected to take certain things into consideration, his action is not immoral; but if we believe that he should have considered them in making his decision, we will regard him as having acted immorally.

I am sure that any ethical or legal theorist could add to this list of forms of immorality. But this list gives us an insight into the major weaknesses of the personality that give rise to immoral behaviour: weakness of will, obsession with demonic values, forgetfulness, unrestrained emotionalism, carelessness and negligence, failure to appreciate the importance of the ideals of civilization.

The immorality of intolerance can take any of these forms. There are men who want to be tolerant but are the slaves of their emotions, of trivial desires, or of the demonic elements in their personality. There are men who have chosen to pursue intolerance along with other demonic 'ideals' (for instance, destruction, violence). There are men who are so preoccupied with other things that they forget about their obligation to consider the interests of men of other faiths. Consider these examples. 1 / Mr R has nothing against Roman Catholics, and he knows that it is wrong to discriminate against them. Yet, he is afraid that if he fraternizes with his Catholic neighbours or allows his children to play with Catholic children, the influential anti-Catholics in his community will make trouble for him, and his business will suffer. He hates himself for participating in anti-Catholic actions, but he is too weak-willed to stop doing so. 2 / Mr S cannot control the destructive side of his personality. He abuses his wife, ignores his children, picks fights with his neighbours and co-workers, makes life miserable for his employees, and refuses to hire anyone but white, Anglo-Saxon Protestants. He gets strange satisfaction out of being universally disliked. 3 / Bishop T is so resentful of liberal Protestant defences of abortion on demand that he urges his flock to boycott all businesses owned by non-Catholics. When the visiting archbishop reminds Bishop T of the importance of loving one's neighbour, T apologizes and admits that his boycott idea was not a good one. 4 / Mr U's compassion for blacks leads him to support legislation that is indirectly harmful to members of other minorities, including religious ones. 5 / Mr V, a well-meaning Protestant, votes in the city council to give tax support to Roman Catholic schools. Only later does he realize that this policy will put an additional economic burden on struggling

Lutheran and Jewish schools. Though basically a 'nice' man, v consistently votes without having considered all of the major effects of the policies he supports.

Here we can see the range of psychological factors that predispose men to be intolerant. Some are more important than others; being barbarous is a whole lot worse than being forgetful or careless. But we can see that it is wrong to isolate one or two psychological factors and hold them up as 'the' causes of all religious intolerance. The problem of religious intolerance has many dimensions, non-psychological as well as psychological; and the psychological dimension of the problem is as complex as the phenomenon of immorality itself.

INTOLERANCE AND SELF-RESPECT

In an earlier chapter, we saw Gordon Allport argue that 'bigotry enters only when religion becomes the apologist for in-group superiority and overextends itself by disparaging out-groups for reasons that extend beyond deviation in creed.' I have explained why Allport's theory of religious intolerance is one-dimensional and hence unsatisfactory; but I have also admitted that Allport *has* put his finger on *one* source of religious intolerance. It is an important one, though Allport is hardly the first person to have noticed it. At some level of consciousness, all people seek self-realization, self-fulfilment. Everyone wants to believe that his life is in some way 'meaningful,' that he has accomplished something. Nobody is willing to believe that he is wholly unimportant, that his life does not matter to anyone. People want to have respect for themselves, to feel competent, to be 'somebodies.' People evaluate themselves by weighing their achievements. They compare their achievements to those of other men, and they seek the approval and praise of other men. Every major philosopher and psychologist has recognized the importance of man's desire for honour, fame, and prestige. An important twentieth-century psychologist, Freud's wayward disciple Alfred Adler, has argued that the *driving force* behind human behaviour is not, as Freud thought, sexuality, but a desire to overcome feelings of inferiority. Centuries earlier, Hobbes had pointed out that the only motive stronger than vanity is fear of death. In ancient times, Plato and Aristotle had to present arguments against the view that honour is the highest good. And the Pentateuch shows us Korah and his arrogant associates challenging the leadership of Moses: 'Ye take too much upon you, seeing all the congregation are holy, every one of them, and the Lord is among them; wherefore then lift ye up yourselves above the assembly of the Lord?' (Numbers 16:3).

The point of all this is that human beings have always had – and will always have – a psychological need for self-respect. Sometimes this need for self-respect manifests itself in positive ways. Men do wonderful things in order to gain self-respect and the respect of others. Sometimes, however, the need for self-respect manifests itself in negative ways. Men have been known to do all sorts of stupid, terrible things in order to make themselves feel important or in order to be noticed by their fellow human beings. (It is a sobering thought that Adolf Hitler is considerably more famous than Albert Schweitzer; and winners of the Nobel Peace Prize are rarely as famous as mindless Hollywood starlets, football players, or political hacks.) One way in which people derive self-respect is by looking down on outsiders, by 'disparaging out-groups.' Since many people think that religion is a very important thing, perhaps the most important thing in human life (and even after), we should not be surprised at the large number of people who derive their self-respect from their belief that they are superior to men who do not share their religious views and their religious way of life. Unfortunately, as we have seen, men are not usually content with just *feeling* superior. They often try to make their 'superiority' known in the most bizarre and barbarous ways.

We have to show people that they should only respect themselves for the *good* things that they do. We have to get them to manifest their need for self-respect in healthy, constructive ways. We have to encourage people to worry more about doing the right thing than doing something that will bring them honour and fame. We could begin by reading to them this passage from Aristotle's *Nicomachean Ethics*: 'Yet honour is surely too superficial a thing to be the good we are seeking. Honour depends more on those who confer than on him who receives it, and we cannot but feel that the good is something personal and almost inseparable from its possessor. Again, why do men seek honour? Surely in order to confirm the favourable opinion they have formed of themselves. It is at all events by intelligent men who know them personally that they seek to be honoured. And for what? For their moral qualities.'[3] From time to time, we should read this passage to ourselves too.

How are we to cope with the 'psychological' sources of religious intolerance? Do we need some kind of mass psychotherapy? Perhaps, but not the kind of psychotherapy that we associate with wealthy physicians. For except in certain special cases, what is called for here is the most obvious of all cures for the sickness of the psyche. This cure is very old and is identical with the preventive, an ounce of which is worth a pound of cure. We call it 'moral education.' Long before there was a Sigmund Freud or a B.F. Skinner or a Gordon Allport, it was being liberally dispensed by such gifted men as Moses, Buddha, Plato, and Jesus of Nazareth.

9

Education for tolerance

Enlightened people are constantly searching for radical solutions to grave social problems. In our society, there are so many problems – crime, unemployment, inflation, violence, war, exploitation (to name just a few) – that we often forget about some of the more insidious obstacles to civilization. The problem of religious intolerance is a grave social problem; now more than ever, religious hatred is at work spreading misery, not only for the people of our time but for future generations. Leftists tell us that as soon as the revolution comes, all our social problems will suddenly begin to disappear. Humanity has seen countless revolutions come and go; most of them seem to have done more harm than good. Whatever progress the human race has made over the centuries (in spite of dreadful lapses into barbarism) has largely been the result of the laborious but effective process of moral education.

In a sense, education *is* civilization. To be educated is to become more civilized. To educate someone is to help him to realize ideals. And one of the major functions of an educational institution is to foster tolerance.

TWO CONFLICTING AIMS OF MORAL EDUCATION

Let us concentrate our attention on the educational institution that stands out the most, the school. The modern school (primary or secondary; public, private, or religious) has two obligations in the area of moral education that cannot be easily reconciled: to socialize and to foster tolerance. (To 'socialize' is to make students appreciate the values of their particular social, cultural, or religious group; to 'foster tolerance' is to get students to accept [the ways of] men of other faiths.) The modern educator is expected to socialize his students – render them social or sociable – by leading them to appreciate the intrinsic and utilitarian merit of the principles, institutions, and values of the particular society to which he and the students belong. Teachers in New York City are hired to explain the value of the presidential system of government, free trade, relative separation of church and state, and so forth. Teachers in Toronto are hired to explain, among other things, the value of the parliamentary system of government, British traditions, and biculturalism. Teachers in Kiev are hired to explain the value of Marxist-Leninist principles. Similarly, teachers in Roman Catholic schools are expected to help their students to be good, devout Catholics, while teachers in the yeshivas, the Jewish schools, are expected to strengthen rather than undermine their students' commitment to Jewish values and the Jewish way of life. Local school-boards and administrators permit teachers to criticize certain traditions and values of their own particular community, but only within limits.

This socialization is defended primarily on the grounds that it promotes communal stability or unity and enables young people to succeed in the political or religious community in which they will probably one day participate as full-fledged members. The fact that these young people are not being prepared to succeed in other political or religious communities is underplayed. Yet, the modern educator is also expected to foster tolerance among his students. He is supposed to show his students, among other things, that though other people may not share our beliefs or ways of doing things, they are not necessarily stupid, wicked, or even misguided. Teachers are mainly encouraged to show the importance of tolerating people within our particular community; but they are not discouraged from imparting to their students a respect for the institutions and values of other communities, even those that are rather different from our own. Indeed students are taught that tolerance is itself one of the most important values of our political or religious community.

It is rarely suggested to teachers that these two tasks, socializing and fostering tolerance, may not be reconcilable. On the surface it appears that they are. One can believe that the institutions and values of one's community are basically sound without believing that they are the *only* possible sound institutions and values. One can also believe that though our institutions and values are generally sound, some of them are not so sound, and we would do well to import certain institutions and values from other societies. (A Catholic, for example, may say to one of his co-religionists, 'I wish we spent more time studying the Bible in the way that Protestants do.')

But consider some other facts. First, two institutions or values or principles may be diametrically opposed; not all are simply alternative means to common ends (except in a very abstract sense). It is not hard for a teacher in New York City to foster tolerance of Canadian or British institutions, but it is much harder for him to foster tolerance of basic Soviet or Chinese institutions. Similarly, a Unitarian teacher can get his students to see that there is some value in certain uniquely Roman Catholic institutions, but his Unitarianism forces him to try to make them regard certain other Catholic institutions as pernicious. At some level, effective socialization requires persuading young people not to tolerate certain institutions, values, and principles of other political or religious communities. If a young person grows up believing that the value-system of the Maoist is not substantially worse (by some standard) than our own, he has not been effectively socialized, and he cannot be expected to defend or even respect 'our' value-system when it is attacked by radicals or reactionaries. The Unitarian teacher is not only teaching his students not to *respect* certain Catholic institutions; he wants them to join him in condemning some of them and in fighting against certain Catholic influences on national policy.

Secondly, the weaknesses of our system (or any other) are not superficial, and this fact is apparent not only to most teachers but also to a good many advanced students. In the primary schools, teachers have relatively little trouble convincing their pupils that, say, the Canadian political system or the Roman Catholic view of church-state relations is basically sound while racial prejudice and social injustice are bad. Older students, being conscious of the relationship between national / church politics and social injustice, are more inclined to be tolerant of Marxist or liberal Protestant values than their younger brothers in the primary schools. Students who are no longer 'ethnocentric' cannot easily be restrained from tolerating values and principles that they were at one time told are intolerable. Many teachers lack the enthusiasm or the intellectual ability necessary for persuading sophisticated students that 'our' institutions and values are genuinely preferable to (or even as good as) those of other political or religious communities. In a sense, then, fostering tolerance involves a kind of 'desocialization.' It *indirectly* promotes relativism, for once a student has learned to put up with something, it is much easier for him to go on to respect it. On this point, at least, the Knoxes and Lippmanns are right.

Now, school-boards and administrators expect teachers to socialize and desocialize simultaneously; yet, 1 / they cannot force teachers to be enthusiastic about the institutions and values that they have been hired to defend; 2/they do not provide teachers with sufficient rational 'apparatus' (that is, good reasons and arguments) for effectively socializing older, sophisticated students; 3 / they accept indoctrination as an alternative to rational justification for those cases where rational justification is impossible or very difficult, even though indoctrination is at odds with the values of tolerance and rationality; and 4/ they do not provide teachers with an adequate method for distinguishing, either for themselves or for their students, between unjustified intolerance (of, for example, the parliamentary system, or the Catholic's worshipping in his own church) and justified 'intolerance' (of, say, neo-Fascism, or Catholic attacks on religious freedom).

Conservative educational theorists like I.L. Kandel have argued that the teacher is the agent of the state and that the teacher's main responsibility in the area of moral education is to *transmit* the ideology, value-system, and cultural heritage of his society to the students. (Religious conservatives argue that the religious teacher is the agent of his church and that his main responsibility in the area of moral education is to transmit the values of the church to his students.) Radical educational theorists, with an eye on corruption and hypocrisy in state and church, have argued that conservative educational theory is dated and that teachers must play an important role in the *reform* of the political or religious community. Conservatives emphasize the teacher's obligation to socialize; radicals emphasize the teacher's obligation to desocialize. In recent years, 'liberal' educational theorists, following Dewey, have believed that they have found a reasonable balance between the two obligations. But have they? In the eyes of both conservatives and radicals, 'liberal' educational theorists are simply confused and indecisive.

Conservatives believe that schools not only *should* mirror society but actually *do*. At the same time they believe that teachers have a responsibility to socialize their students, especially because no individual instructor should take it upon himself to determine what in his community is 'really' good and what is 'really' bad. But if the schools truly mirror society, then desocialization must be on the rise. We saw in earlier chapters that relativism is very much on the rise in intellectual circles. The relativism of intellectuals has gradually been filtering down into other segments of society. Since educational changes generally reflect intellectual changes of an earlier period, and since the recent attack on relativism has not been a very strong one, we are now witnessing the influence of relativistic theories in the schools. We are witnessing the emergence of a generation of young adults who are relatively tolerant and flexible but confused and devoid of firm moral commitments. 'Moral weakness' is on the rise. Critics of relativism and modern educational theory argue that the time has come for the schools to return to the job of vigorously socializing, even if doing so will lead to the next generation's being less tolerant and flexible than its predecessor. But must we return to a conservative educational theory, or is there another alternative?

TWO KINDS OF SOCIALIZATION

We have seen that there can be tolerance without relativism; and we have also seen the importance of the idea of civilization. Let us think of education as the civilizing process. Many educational theorists have pointed out that education involves more than simply *changing* a person. Education involves changing a person in such a way as to make him a *better* person. The term 'education' has a normative aspect as well as a descriptive one. So education is not simply socialization in the sense of making young people fit into a society, appreciate the society's institutions and values, obey its ethical code, and so forth. After all, most of us believe that 'teachers' in a state like Nazi Germany do not *educate* young people. They train, condition, indoctrinate, *socialize*, but they do not educate.

If education is socialization, then, it is a special kind of socialization. It is not simply a matter of promoting social stability or even enabling people to be 'successful' in the context of one particular society; it is not simply a matter of getting people to be very much like the other people in that particular society. When we say that a man is an educated man, we are not simply saying that he now has beliefs, values, and dispositions that are *different* from those he had before; we are saying that he now has beliefs, values, and dispositions that are *better* than those he had before and are closer to those *all* men *ought* to have. And so we can say that men are educated even when they come from a society or religious group that is significantly different from our own. A truly educated man is one who has not simply been socialized but has been socialized in a special way. An educated man is one who has been civilized. Education does not simply make a man a better American, a better Catholic, a better Nazi, or a better devil-worshipper. It makes a man a better person, a better human being.

Conservative educational theorists rightly argue that the single most important obligation of the educator is to socialize his students. If we foster toleration among our students to the point where they have no absolute moral values (and no *belief* in the *existence* of absolute moral values), then they may end up with a 'moral' code that is not much better than the barbarian's. Moreover, we have left them in a state where they are as susceptible to the influence of the propaganda of barbarism as to that of the propaganda of civilization. However, radical educators who are *dogmatic*, and are trying to peddle their own pet values, can be as dangerous as those who are relativistic. Conservative educational theorists are justified in observing that we cannot always trust sincere educators who have taken it upon themselves to decide for their students what is absolutely right and what is absolutely wrong. Still, the fact that certain beliefs and values already *prevail* in the educator's own political or religious community in no way establishes that those beliefs and values are good for his students to hold. Bad socializing is as dangerous as radical desocializing. Radical educational theorists, pointing to the deep-rooted weaknesses of the community to which they belong, see most socialization in the schools as indoctrination through propaganda. Yet, their alternative to propaganda is different propaganda, the propaganda of relativism or of some unfashionable ideology.

The liberal educational theorist must find some way of steering a middle course between the narrow socialization of the conservative (which promotes intolerance) and the excessive relativism of the genuine, non-dogmatic radical (which promotes 'moral weakness'). It is not enough to believe that such a course is possible; one must see some philosophical basis for it. Here is where it is important that we recognize that education is the process of civilizing. Bad socialization and radical desocialization do not change young people for the better and so they cannot be proper educational methods. Civilizing cannot be bad socializing. Civilization is a good thing, as is civility or being civilized. If education is the process of civilizing, then to educate people is to assist them to realize, mainly by means of reason, a large number of trans-cultural ideals (for instance, love, peace, justice, and wisdom), not only for themselves, but for their fellow creatures too. Of course, people can civilize themselves; a person can be 'self-educated.' But an educator can help others, both in his own society and in other societies, to realize more ideals more rapidly.

When an educator civilizes people, he makes them better citizens of their state and better members of their religious community – better

Canadians, better Brazilians, better Moslems, better Presbyterians, and so on. He also encourages them to be reasonably tolerant and flexible, to respect the rights of men in other communities, to put up with outsiders who pose no serious threat to civilization. He thus satisfies the demands of both conservative educational theorists and radical ones. But he does more: he encourages his students to repudiate institutions and policies that conflict with the trans-cultural moral ideals, whether they be institutions and policies endorsed by outsiders or by the leaders of their own state or church. He helps them to see, for example, why they should admire their state or church for its charitable endeavours and why they should not condone its refusal to speak out against racism and economic exploitation. He helps them to see that they can learn from outsiders but should not accept the evils of other communities as mere 'cultural' differences. In short, educational institutions are proper and vital instruments of socialization, but only if socialization is understood as civilization. And if institutions are to be effective instruments of civilization, they must not only encourage belief in the existence of absolute moral values, but they must help young people (and older ones too) to understand the trans-cultural values and how they may be realized most quickly and most efficiently.

We may now descend from philosophical abstractions to concrete conditions. A child in primary school in North America is relatively uncivilized, relatively low on the scale of civilization. He is not what we would normally call a 'savage' or 'barbarian,' because even if he is dominated by the demonic elements in his personality, he belongs to a family and a community that are themselves dominated by people who are relatively high on the scale of civilization, and in time, with proper education, he too will take his place as a highly civilized member of a highly civilized community. But still he must be regarded as relatively uncivilized, uneducated; he is not wholly rational (or even close to being so), he sees few 'outsiders' as having rights, and he has extremely naïve conceptions of love, justice, wisdom, beauty, and so forth. He does not really understand his way of life but is drifting along under the (often inadequate) direction of his parents and friends. But if his human nature has *determined* that when he has grown up his basic ideals will be love, justice, and so on, then why is it necessary for the school to get into the business of moral education? The answer is that the school does not so much expose the student to new values (though it may occasionally do so) as deepen his understanding of the positive values he already holds. A ten-year-old child does have ideas about love, justice, wisdom, and beauty; but they are naïve, confused, and inconsistent. In many cases, children pick up such ideas from adults whose ideas about trans-cultural values are naïve, confused, and inconsistent.

Consider the case of a ten-year-old child who steals a pen from a class-mate. If he could articulate clearly what he regards as the justification of his act, he might tell us, 'I need the pen more than my class-mate does because his parents are wealthier than mine,' or 'My parents have told me that sometimes it is all right to steal, especially when no one is hurt very much.' When the teacher tells this child about justice and fairness, it will not be the first time that the child has been lectured to about justice and fairness. Undoubtedly he has been told about the importance of justice and fairness by the very same parents who have encouraged him to be aggressive and prudent. The teacher has to *sharpen* the student's conception of justice; he has to make it less abstract in the student's mind. Five years later, the student's defence of theft will be more sophisticated. It will probably have a Machiavellian or a Hobbesian twist: 'Everyone steals. My parents cheat on their income taxes. Politicians exploit people both at home and abroad. My teachers draw a nice salary while being pretty much unconcerned with the oppressed peoples of the world. All these people who always lecture me about justice are hypocrites. To get by in this world, one has to be aggressive and bend some rules.' Again, the teacher's obligation here is to sharpen his student's conception of justice. He has to show the student that it is necessary to distinguish the absolute value of justice, which is an ideal to be realized, from the 'shadows' of justice that have been placed before him by hypocritical parents, politicians, clergymen, teachers, television personalities, and other sophists. To counter his cynicism, the teacher must appeal to simple rational arguments of the utilitarian or deontological kind.

I would describe positive values in much the same way as John Stuart Mill has described what he calls 'moral feelings.' They are not innate, but they are natural:

If, as is my own belief, the moral feelings are not innate but acquired, they are not for that reason the less natural. It is natural to man to speak, to reason, to build cities, to cultivate the ground, though these are acquired faculties ... Like the other acquired capacities above referred to, the moral faculty, if not a part of our nature, is a natural outgrowth from it; capable, like them, in a certain, small degree, of springing up spontaneously; and susceptible of being brought by cultivation to a high degree of development.[1]

When we look at the large number of students in secondary schools and universities who are disenchanted with our 'system' and attracted to exotic, radical political ideologies and religious outlooks, we should immediately be reminded of the weaknesses of the kind of socialization that the conservative educational theorists defend. When the child of ten is told that his state or church can do no wrong, he has no reason to believe that the people who are telling him this are liars. When, at the age of fifteen or sixteen, he sees that the weaknesses of this community's codes and institutions have been hidden from him, he may well over-react, by becoming either radical or just cynical. If, however, he has been socialized so 'successfully' that he cannot see any weakness in his community's codes and institutions, then he is now morally blind and incapable of criticizing evils in his own society. Bad socialization can lead, then, to hatred of one's own community or hatred of other societies. It can produce the worst intolerance.

But how can the educator sharpen his students' conceptions of love, justice, and other trans-cultural values? Traditionally, his main tool for civilizing has been the study and discussion of great literary works. When I was in school, I was required to read such books as *Arrowsmith*, *Hiroshima*, *The Good Earth*, *King Lear*, *Macbeth*, and *David Copperfield*. Though these works vary in aesthetic quality, they all force us to reflect on moral questions and deepen our understanding of ethical ideals. When I was older, I was ready for works like *Faust*, *Don Quijote*, *Hamlet*, the novels of Kafka, and the ancient Greek tragedies. Eventually I was able to understand works of moral philosophy and Oriental literature. (I am afraid that today's young people are being fed on a diet of nihilistic books and films.) At each stage of my reading, I came to realize that: 1 / there is a limited number of ultimate human aspirations; 2 / great thinkers of all backgrounds have remarkably similar ideas about these aspirations; 3 / it is possible to have a deeper understanding of justice, beauty, and so on than I used to have; 4 / many people that I once trusted use terms like 'love' and 'justice' far too promiscuously and uncritically; and 5 / there are alternative ways of approximating any particular ideal, and some appear to be better than others.

Another tool for civilizing has been the study and discussion of history. Also, it is usually in school that one first learns how to appreciate a painting, a symphony, and a poem, how to keep himself in good physical condition, what to look for in a walk through the country or the city. In other words, one is not only taught what to avoid; one is also shown how many positive things life has to offer. This kind of socialization not only enriches a student's experience but enables him to distinguish between what is truly good and truly bad in any human community, including our own. It enables a student to avoid both the narrow-mindedness of ethnocentrism and the cynical aimlessness of relativism. As for the 'civics' that was forced upon me in primary school, I doubt whether it still exerts much influence upon my moral and political judgment.

And of all the tools for civilizing, none is more important than the study and discussion of works of religious literature. It is the holy books of men of all faiths that most powerfully and most directly draw our attention to the highest spiritual ideals, the noblest aspirations, the potential greatness that is open to a man who sincerely strives to realize these ideals and aspirations. These hortatory works summon us to choose the course of civilization rather than the course of barbarism, to choose good over evil. And for this reason, religion and education go hand in hand and complement one another. How, people often ask, can something as noble, as civilizing, as uplifting as religion have brought the human community so much misery? I have given a few answers to this question, but surely none is as important as this one: religious teachers have rarely modelled themselves after the greatest and noblest religious teachers, those *prophets* whom they have falsely professed to be following. Nor is incompetence uniquely characteristic of *religious* teachers. Even in our highly civilized society, we have entrusted second-rate minds with the most important vocation in any state or church, that of civilizing. And why should gifted men be attracted to the teaching profession? Our teachers are, for the most part, undervalued, unappreciated, and discouraged. What a pity! The competent educator not only deepens his students' understanding of the highest ideals but helps them to be rational, to see through sophistical arguments, to avoid prejudice.

And so, if you ask me what the most effective preventive and cure of religious intolerance is, I can only answer, 'Education.' I am not referring here to the bad socialization that is often passed off as education. I am referring to the genuine article, a process of civilizing. I realize that this answer is not very original. It is an answer the great prophets and philosophers have given over and over again. Unfortunately, it is an answer that is forgotten over and over again. And so it must be repeated over and over again.

PROSPECTS

Religious intolerance survives (and in some places actually *thrives*) largely because few people who are in a position to do something about it are willing to see it as constituting a 'major' social problem. In the view of many liberal intellectuals, religious intolerance is, for all intents and purposes, a 'dead issue'; for not only are the days of the auto-da-fé, the Crusades, and the holy wars long gone, but other, more immediate problems command our attention. Liberal intellectuals are so preoccupied with problems of economic injustice, racism, political repression, corruption, and world hunger that they simply cannot find time to worry about the fact that religious intolerance is still around, rearing its ugly head. But someone ought to be worrying about religious intolerance, and if the liberal intellectual will not worry about it, who will? The bigot? The fanatic?

Those who underestimate the importance of the ancient and continuing problem of religious intolerance are terribly short-sighted. There is still relatively little religious liberty in the world. Even in highly civilized societies like our own, unwarranted religious discrimination is far from uncommon. Moreover, religious intolerance is often a source, component, or by-product of other social evils. I shall go out on a limb here and suggest that the *majority* of contemporary social problems have *some* sort of religious connection or aspect.

While we can see, then, that religious intolerance is but one of many contemporary social problems, we can still wonder why it does not receive more attention than it does. Allow me to suggest some possible explanations. 1 / Many liberal intellectuals have deceived themselves into believing that religion is a dying phenomenon. They believe that as religion gradually disappears, religious intolerance will die out with it. Since these people regard intolerance as an inevitable concomitant of religious faith, they believe that the best way to fight religious intolerance is to minimize the influence of religion in social life. And liberal atheistic intellectuals have waged a clever war against religion. Atheistic journalists appreciate the value of *ignoring* religion; atheistic professors make crude jokes about it. They do these things largely because in their view the tolerant man must be an enemy of religion per se. But these men are very naïve. For not only do they wrongly see religion as an intrinsically pernicious phenomenon, but they fail to appreciate its continuing importance as a form of human experience. They assume that because they and their élitist friends have no use for religion, serious religious commitment cannot survive long. They are mistaken. Many churches are empty; many religious denominations are struggling – financially, politically, and philosophically. Yet, religion is here to stay. Over the centuries it has had its ups and downs. But people keep coming back to it. It satisfies intellectual and emotional needs that no other form of experience can satisfy. It will take new forms, but it will always return. So those liberal intellectuals who think that religion and religious intolerance will just peter out are very poor students of human nature.

2 / Because many liberal intellectuals are wedded to narrow, one-dimensional ideologies, they cannot recognize religious intolerance *for what it is*. They want to explain it *away*. For Allport, religious intolerance has relatively little to do with religion; he sees it as largely a matter of in-group safety-seeking. Allport's view is more subtle than most. Journalists shamelessly feed us the myth that the Catholics and Protestants who are blowing themselves up in Ireland disagree on issues that are basically *economic*. Others tell us that the conflicts in the Middle East are purely *political*, battles over territory. Well-meaning but ignorant commentators tell us that anti-Semitism has very little to do with religion and is basically a kind of racism. Some of these people are simply afraid to criticize 'religion'; but most refuse to take religion as seriously as it deserves to be taken.

3 / Many liberal intellectuals have left it to 'ecumenical leaders' to solve the problem of religious intolerance. If they refuse to leave it to liberal economists to solve economic problems, or to liberal politicians to solve political problems, why should they be so willing to trust 'ecumenical leaders'? The fact is that the ecumenical movement, which began in a blaze of glory, has had its problems, especially of late. Many 'ecumenical leaders' are atheists or relativists, and religious traditionalists do not trust them. Though it has some important achievements to its credit, the ecumenical movement has spawned almost as many concrete problems as it has solved. Unfortunately, the ecumenical movement has to a great extent come to be associated with radical theological movements.

4 / Many liberal intellectuals are themselves intolerant men. I have met very few non-Catholic academics who are not at least mildly anti-Catholic; though some academic hostility towards Catholicism and Catholics is understandable or even justifiable, much of it is not. And many liberal intellectuals are irrationally hostile towards religious people in general. Many of these people are, consciously or

unconsciously, *pleased* by the continuing existence of religious intoler-ance, for it confirms their worst opinions of Catholics or Christians or religious people in general. So while they speak out forcefully against interference by the churches in secular matters, they often condone the persecution of religious minorities.

5 / The content of academic or journalistic discussion depends largely on what happens to be in fashion. Right now, the subject of religious intolerance is not a fashionable one to discuss; today liberals have decided to be guilt-ridden about x, and tomorrow they will be guilt-ridden about y. Yes, the days of the auto-da-fé are long gone; but as far as most men are concerned, so are the days of Belsen and Treblinka. How many people can tell you what happened at Belsen and Treblinka?

The reflective man is tempted to become very pessimistic. It is a temptation that he must avoid. For as we have seen, those who dwell on the morbid, on the negative, are succumbing to domination by the demonic elements of their personality. The writings of cynics, 'realists,' and negativists have done little to help solve concrete human problems. It is healthier to be an optimist than a pessimist. (I have in mind here a cautious optimism, not a blind, paralysing one.) Those of us who are not armed with an optimistic *eschatology* still have a moral obligation to believe that further civilization – further *civilizing* – is possible. If the prospects for religious tolerance are not bright, then it is our business as human beings to *make* them bright. No matter what his eschatology, a human being must come to grips with the fact of his responsibility, and one of his most basic responsibilities is to exemplify and promote tolerance. 'Ah,' you may say, 'but it is so hard to be tolerant, and the problem of intolerance is so complex, and how can we avoid being cynical and pessimistic?' Reflect, then, on the words of the greatest of all champions of religious tolerance, that most persecuted of philosophers, Spinoza: 'But all things that are excellent are as difficult as they are rare.'[2]

Notes

CHAPTER 1

1 See, for instance, George W. Spicer, *The Supreme Court and Fundamental Freedoms* (New York : Appleton-Century-Crofts 1959), 60–77; William H. Marnell, *The First Amendment* (Garden City, NY: Doubleday 1964), 173–83.
2 Aristotle, *Nicomachean Ethics,* 1110a, trans. by W.D. Ross (Oxford: Clarendon Press 1925)

CHAPTER 2

1 Gordon W. Allport, *The Nature of Prejudice* (Cambridge, Mass.: Addison-Wesley Publishing Company 1954), 6–7
2 Ibid., 444
3 William James, *The Varieties of Religious Experience* (London and New York: Longmans, Green 1904 [1902]), lecture 14, p. 338
4 Etienne Gilson, *Reason and Revelation in the Middle Ages* (New York: Scribner's 1938), 96

5 See James, *Varieties of Religious Experience.*

CHAPTER 3

1 See, for instance, Paul Tillich, *Dynamics of Faith* (New York: Harper and Row 1958), 55–73.
2 In a sense, almost all works of philosophy and social science are indirectly attacks on relativism.
3 A wide range of theories about metaphysics have been taken to be relativistic. Here are some of them. 1 / Metaphysical principles are not true or false; rather, they are absolute presuppositions, rules, categorial principles, or organizing concepts. 2 / Metaphysical beliefs are hypotheses that we accept on the basis of pragmatic criteria. 3 / Metaphysical beliefs are true for one person and false for another. 4 / Metaphysical theories are aesthetic objects.

4 F.C.S. Schiller, *Must Philosophers Disagree? and Other Essays in Popular Philosophy* (London: Macmillan 1934), 11–12, 163

5 See H.P. Rickman's translation of excerpts from Dilthey's writings, *Pattern and Meaning in History* (London: George Allen and Unwin 1961), ch. 6.

6 William James, 'The Will to Believe,' in *The Will to Believe and Other Essays in Popular Philosophy* (New York: Longmans, Green 1907), 13–14

7 Gabriel Marie Cardinal Garrone, 'To the Ordinaries of the World on the Study of Philosophy in Seminaries,' *Sacra Congregatio Pro Institutione Catholica*, Prot. N. 137/65 (1972)

8 Benedetto Croce, 'Eternal Truth,' in *My Philosophy*, trans. by E.F. Carritt (London: George Allen and Unwin 1949), 222

9 Benedetto Croce, 'My Philosophy,' Ibid., 11

10 R.G. Collingwood, *An Essay on Metaphysics* (Oxford: Clarendon Press 1940), 225–6

11 *Must Philosophers Disagree?* 12

12 Melville J. Herskovits, *Man and His Works* (New York: Alfred A. Knopf 1964 [1948]), 63. Cf. pp. 61–78.

13 Defined by Herskovits as 'the manmade part of the environment' (ibid., 17).

14 Ibid., 71

15 See R.G. Collingwood, *The New Leviathan* (Oxford: Clarendon Press 1942), pt. 3.

16 *The Speeches of Adolf Hitler*, passages ed. and trans. by Norman H. Baynes (New York: Howard Fertig, 1969), I, 573, speech of 11 September 1935

17 *The Bhagavad Gita*, trans. by Juan Mascaró (Harmondsworth, Eng.: Penguin Books 1962), 2.33, 2.66

18 *The Sayings of Confucius*, trans. by James R. Ware (New York: The New American Library 1955), 4.16, 14.24

19 Clyde Kluckhohn, 'Ethical Relativity: *Sic et Non*,' *Journal of Philosophy*, 52 (1955), 672–3. On p. 671, Kluckhohn writes that '[Ralph] Linton is squarely in the mainstream of contemporary anthropological opinion when he says: "Behind the seemingly endless diversity of culture patterns there is a fundamental uniformity."' Cf. Franz Boas, *The Mind of Primitive Man* (2nd ed.; New York: Free Press 1965 [1911, 1938]), ch. 11; Clark Wissler, *Man and Culture* (New York: Thomas Y. Crowell 1923), ch. 5.

20 Edward Westermarck, *Ethical Relativity* (New York: Harcourt, Brace 1932), 197. Cf. Morris Ginsberg, *On the Diversity of Morals* (London: Royal Anthropological Institute of Great Britain and Ireland, 1953).

21 *Man and His Works*, 76

22 *The Speeches of Adolf Hitler*, ed.

and trans. by Baynes (see 16 above).

23 *Ethical Relativity*

CHAPTER 4

1 R.A. Knox, *The Belief of Catholics* (London: Ernest Benn 1927), 241–3
2 Walter Lippmann, *A Preface to Morals* (New York: Macmillan, 1929), 74–6
3 Ibid., 76–8
4 Ibid., 82–3

CHAPTER 5

1 C.E.M. Joad, 'Thought and Temperament,' in *Essays in Commonsense Philosophy* (Port Washington, NY: Kennikat Press 1969 [1920]), 251–2
2 The distinction between 'act-utilitarianism' and 'rule-utilitarianism' may be summarized as follows. According to act-utilitarianism, a person should perform that act which will result in the greatest good for the greatest number; according to rule-utilitarianism, a person should follow that rule which will result in the greatest good for the greatest number. See, e.g., Paul W. Taylor, *Principles of Ethics: An Introduction* (Encino, Calif.: Dickenson 1975), 63–8.
3 Dale Carnegie, *How to Win Friends and Influence People* (New York: Simon and Schuster 1937), 139

4 *Utrum sit cum infidelibus publice disputandum.* The text and translation used throughout are those of the Blackfriars, vol. 32, ed. Thomas Gilby, O.P. (London: Eyre and Spottiswoode; New York: McGraw-Hill 1975).
5 *Si enim disputet tanquam de fide dubitans ... procul dubio peccat, tanquam dubius in fide et infidelis. Si autem disputet aliquis de fide ad confutandum errores, vel etiam ad exercitium, laudabile est.*
6 *Inordinatam, quae magis fit contentione verborum quam firmitate sententiarum.*
7 *Propter veritatem manifestandam et errores confutandos ... ad convincendos errantes.*
8 *Malis persuasionibus.*
9 Cecil Roth, 'The European Age in Jewish History (to 1648),' in Louis Finkelstein ed, *The Jews: Their History* (4th ed.; New York: Schocken Books 1970), 244

CHAPTER 6

1 Nicolas Berdyaev, *The Fate of Man in the Modern World*, trans. by Donald A. Lowrie (Ann Arbor: University of Michigan Press 1961 [1935]), 100
2 Ibid., 101
3 Edward A. Synan, *The Popes and the Jews in the Middle Ages* (New York: Macmillan 1965), 1
4 Ibid., 3
5 Nicholas Wiseman, *Lectures on*

the *Principal Doctrines and Practices of the Catholic Church* (2nd ed.; Baltimore: John Murphy 1846), I, 275–6

6 Louis Finkelstein, *The Pharisees: The Sociological Background of Their Faith* (3rd ed.; Philadelphia: Jewish Publication Society of America, 1962), I, 145–6

7 John Calvin, *Institutes of the Christian Religion*, ed. John T. McNeill, trans. by Ford Lewis Battles (Philadelphia: Westminster Press 1960), II, 931 (3.21)

8 Ibid., 937 (3.22)

9 Plato, *Republic*, 367e, trans. by Paul Shorey (London: William Heinemann; New York: G.P. Putman's Sons 1930), I, 145

10 Letter 67, Albert Burgh to Spinoza, 3 September 1675, and Letter 76, Spinoza to Burgh, December 1675, trans. by A. Wolf in *The Correspondence of Spinoza* (London: George Allen and Unwin 1928), 310–24, 350–5

11 Letter 19, Spinoza to Blyenbergh, Wolf trans., ibid., 149–50

12 John Colerus, 'The Life of Benedict de Spinoza,' from an early English translation reprinted in Frederick Pollock, *Spinoza: His Life and Philosophy* (London: Kegan Paul 1880), 421

13 Spinoza, ibid. (n. 10)

CHAPTER 7

1 315 U.S. 571 (1942)

2 Spicer, George W. *The Supreme Court and Fundamental Freedoms* (New York: Appleton-Century-Crofts 1959), 77. 310 U.S. 586 (1940; later overruled), 321 U.S. 158 (1944), 345 U.S. 395 (1953)

3 See, for instance, Sidney Hook, *Religion in a Free Society* (Lincoln: University of Nebraska Press 1967), and Milton R. Konvitz, *Religious Liberty and Conscience* (New York: Viking Press 1968).

4 133 U.S. 342–3 (1890)

5 Philip B. Kurland, *Religion and the Law* (Chicago: Aldine 1962), 24

6 See, for instance, Loren P. Beth, *The American Theory of Church and State* (Gainesville: University of Florida Press 1958), ch. 3

7 In a 1970 survey, almost half of the people questioned said that they believed that the government could not be trusted all of the time. See Richard E. Dawson, *Public Opinion and Contemporary Disarray* (New York: Harper and Row 1973), 47.

8 John Henry Newman, *A Letter of His Grace the Duke of Norfolk* (London: Pickering 1875), part 5. Cf. Konvitz, ibid., ch. 4.

9 U.S. 462 (1961)

10 See, for instance, J.O. Urmson, 'The Interpretation of the Moral Philosophy of J.S. Mill,' *Philosophical Quarterly* 3 (1953), 33–9.

11 Henry Kamen, *The Rise of Toleration* (New York: McGraw-Hill 1967), 7 and passim

CHAPTER 8

1 David Hume, 'Of Superstition and Enthusiasm,' in *Essays, Moral and Political* (Edinburgh: Kincaid 1741)
2 Cf. Aristotle, *Nicomachean Ethics*, 1115b
3 Ibid,. 1095b, trans. by J.A.K. Thomson (London: George Allen and Unwin 1953), 18

CHAPTER 9

1 John Stuart Mill, 'Utilitarianism,' ch. 3 in *Collected Works* (Toronto: University of Toronto Press; Routledge and Kegan Paul 1969), x, 230
2 The last line of the *Ethics* (*Sed omnia praeclara tam difficilia quam rara sunt*).

Index